Writing
and
Personality

Writing and Personality

Finding Your Voice,
Your Style, Your Way

John K. DiTiberio
and
George H. Jensen

Davies-Black Publishing
Palo Alto, California

Published by Davies-Black, a division of Consulting Psychologists Press, Inc., 3803 E. Bayshore Road, Palo Alto, CA 94303, 1-800-624-1765

98 97 96 95   10 9 8 7 6 5 4 3 2 1
Printed in the United States of America

Library of Congress Cataloging-in-Publication Data
DiTiberio, John K.
    Writing and personality : finding your voice, your style, your way / John K. DiTiberio and George H. Jensen. -- 1st ed.
        p.   cm.
    Includes bibliographical references and index.
    ISBN 0-89106-071-5
    1. Authorship.   I. Jensen, George H.   II. Title.
PN151.D58   1995
808'.02—dc20   94–24284
                                                                          CIP

First edition
    First printing, 1995

To Lisa and Donna

Contents

Prologue

When we began working together almost fifteen years ago, we were interested in helping college and graduate students who struggled with academic writing. We soon discovered that writers in all settings, not just students, were most effective when they let their personality guide their writing. We then coauthored articles and eventually a book for professional composition teachers and theorists on how personality relates to the writing process.

What has been lacking is a practical translation of this research and theory to everyday writing situations for everyday writers. People who attend our seminars and workshops tell us that the principles we discovered in university settings have also provided helpful ideas for how to make writing work for them. It is the purpose of this book to bring these ideas to a general audience, whether writing in the workplace, in the classroom, or for publication.

Neither of us, frankly, likes the idea of a how-to book for writers, especially one that takes personality into account. Distinct behaviors and thinking processes are required at different stages of the writing process, for different genres, and in different contexts. Furthermore, personality types can never be reduced to discrete categories, nor can we advocate easy solutions for complex problems simply by knowing a person's "type." We wrote the book to make this complexity involved in writing a bit more understandable.

We do intend, however, for this book to be enjoyable to read. In most chapters, we provide brief exercises to engage your attention and to illustrate how the model works. Periodically, we intersperse tables to summarize key points for easy reference. We also include anecdotes and quotations both from our experiences with writers and from the comments of famous authors.

We are both faculty members at midwestern universities. Our work together and the model in this book emerge from an integration of the two disciplines we work in. John is a counseling psychologist who teaches in an education department. George is a composition specialist in a department of English. George's understanding of how writing is typically taught and John's perspective on how people differ according to Jung's theory of types provided the framework for our first collaborative efforts. A decade and a half later, we find the two languages so compatible that it is now hard to tell which of us originated which application.

In this book, we intend to help all writers make use of knowledge of their personality to understand their preferred writing process and to become more effective writers. We will, of course, deal with typical blocks and anxieties that writers face. However, one of our main points is that troubles with writing often emerge when we abandon the natural processes that come easily to us. Too many writers are "blocked" because they derive their approach mainly from the requirements of the writing task, the person requiring it, or the setting in which it is to be done. In this way we agree with Frank Smith, who said in a book called *Writing and the Writer* that

> writing is always personal (even though what is written may
> not be personal).... Some [writers] need absolute silence and
> freedom from distraction, while others seem able to write in
> any circumstances.... A few seem incapable of writing an
> ungrammatical sentence; others must concentrate on ideas
> first and attend to matters of grammar and style later. Some
> cannot bear to have their writing revised; others are reluctant
> to let it go without multiple revisions. Some flourish under
> deadlines, but many find it impossible to write to order....
> Some can dictate, but many cannot.... Teachers must not
> assume that their own idiosyncrasies are the only
> or even the best way to write.

Our purpose is to help you discover that these differences in writing approaches are not simply random. They illustrate variations in personality that are both interesting and justifiable. We hope to help writers appreciate such *Gifts Differing,* to cite the title of the book by Isabel Myers that has inspired our work.

The book is divided into four parts. In part 1, you will investigate your beginnings and your present as a writer to learn how you came to view writing as you currently do.

Part 2 presents the model of how writing is influenced by personality differences. After a general introduction to the model in chapter 3, each of the next four chapters introduces a separate dimension of personality and how it relates to your writing process.

Part 3 includes a description of the preferred approach to writing of each of the sixteen types of people who emerge from the interaction of the four dimensions of personality.

Part 4 focuses on practical applications—that is, ways to use knowledge of your personality to solve specific problems associated with writing. Topics include your natural style of writing, drafting and revising, how different types grow and develop as writers, anxiety and writer's blocks and how to overcome them, writing for different audiences, and collaborating with others while writing. In the epilogue, we discuss the important distinction between *type* and *stereotype*.

We are indebted to many people who, along the way, have encouraged us to write this book, including colleagues both present and past and our students. Over 100 individuals read and made corrections to the section in part 3 that pertains to their preferred writing process. We would also like to acknowledge all of our former students whose work helped inspire examples used in this book. Special thanks are due to James T. Jones, who supplied the idea about writing in one continuous word used in chapter 1.

Finally, we want to express our gratitude to Lee Langhammer Law, director of book publishing at CPP, for her support for this endeavor, and to Kathleen Hummel, project editor, for her excellent recommendations for how to recraft sections of the book for greater clarity and appeal.

PART I

How Writing Works For You

❧ Both our past and present experiences with writing color how we view ourselves as writers. In the two chapters in this first part of the book, we will ask you to look back at your beginnings as a writer and then examine how you currently go about writing.

Both here and throughout the book we encourage you to keep a notebook and a pen close by as you read. This is because these first two chapters, and several others that follow, include writing exercises designed to help you relate in an active way to the questions we will be raising. Although some of these exercises might seem a little odd at first, we encourage you to give them a chance to tell you about your beginnings as a writer, about your present as a writer, and, in later chapters of the book, about your personality and how it relates to writing.

Your Beginnings
as a Writer

We cannot separate the writer from the writing. Nor should we try. Both our writing process and our writing products need to carry our unique signature, a bit of our personality. In our earliest development as writers, however, many of us treated writing as something quite separate from who we were as growing individuals. The exercises in this first chapter will help you to establish what your beginnings as a writer were like. This will be the starting point for your discovery of natural ways to go about writing that work for you.

How You Learned to Write

We'd like you to take a moment now to think about your first attempts at writing and to write about your earliest memory as a writer. But we would like for you to write in a special way. We want you to write for about ten or fifteen minutes in one continuous word. What we mean by "one continuous word" is that once you begin to write, you should not lift your pen at the end of a word, but continue writing. For example, you might write:

whenIfirstbegantowrite . . .

Do not lift your pen from the page except to move on to the next line. This will help you to get in touch with the physical act of writing—the feel of a pen in your hand and the extended feel of that pen rubbing across paper.

In *Writing Down the Bones: Freeing the Writer Within,* Natalie Goldberg spoke about the physical act of writing in this way:

> Handwriting is more connected to the movement of the heart…. Consider the pen you write with. It should be a fast-writing pen because your thoughts are always faster than your hand. You don't want to slow up your hand even more with a slow pen.

This physical sense of writing, which can tell us so much about how we experience the process of putting words to paper, is often pushed from our consciousness when we concentrate on the meaning we want to convey.

As you write in your continuous word, it is best to leave your t's uncrossed and your i's undotted. That way you can concentrate on the immediate process of forming your letters and constructing words. If you feel a compelling need to cross your t's and dot your i's, try at least to hold off until you reach the end of a line.

What you have done, albeit in a limited way, is to reexperience the process of learning to write. Below is an example of what one adult writer produced as he followed this exercise:

> My earliest memory of trying to write takes me back to first grade even though I knew I was writing long before that. I was very selfconscious about whether I was doing what the teacher wanted us to do in the right way. Even now I want to go back and dot all my i's and cross my t's.

Before this recaptured memory begins to slip away, take some time to reflect on it in another piece of writing. The questions below will help you to think about what this experience has meant to you.

1. How did it feel to hold the pen in your hand and form the letters?
2. What surprised you about this earliest recollection of writing?
3. What were your emotional reactions to writing about this early experience?
4. Do you think that this experience was typical of your early attempts at learning to write, or was it in some way unique?
5. What else do you remember about your early experiences with writing?

The following answers were written by the person who wrote the paragraph for the previous exercise.

1. *It felt awkward. The self-consciousness I was writing about when I was in the first grade was duplicated when I couldn't easily cross my t's or dot my i's or add commas where they were supposed to be.*
2. *It surprised me how quickly I felt like I must have felt in the first grade and how I free associated to the social atmosphere of being in that classroom of classmates and teachers.*
3. *I felt a little embarrassed to discover that in some ways I feel punished inside even today when I start to write.*
4. *I really am not sure if this experience was typical, but I suspect it was.*
5. *I mainly am aware of how important it was to feel connected and supported by people around me when learning a new skill.*

With this exercise, you have begun to reconstruct what learning to write was like for you. It is now time to move from elementary school to high school or college. You will move from how you learned to hold a pen and form letters to how you learned to write book reports, essays, and term papers.

How You See Yourself as a Writer

In order to explore how you began to form your concept of yourself as a writer, we'd like you to try another exercise. We want you to record a simple list of all the feedback, both positive and negative, that you received about your writing in any writing course, whether in high school or college. For example:

- *"Well-written."*
- *"Unclear pronouns—not clear what or who they refer to."*
- *"Too much information and not enough personal integration."*
- *"Too much use of passive voice."*
- *"You need to vary words (use a thesaurus)."*
- *"You need to discuss implications of topic."*
- *"Your writing has vigor."*
- *"Too many misspelled words."*
- *"Too wordy."*
- *"Very thorough."*

If you are the type of person who saves old school papers, you might want to review these to refresh your memory.

After you have made your list of comments that teachers or others have made about your writing, spend ten to fifteen minutes exploring your reactions to these comments. You may go on to explore some of your most vivid memories about writing in high school or college. The following sample shows one writer's reactions to their comments.

I was still very mindful of the personal reactions of teachers and of wanting to do what I could to meet their expectations and to feel both respected and liked by them. Unlike my first-grade memory, I remember feeling somewhat annoyed at teachers who reacted with criticism, some of it feeling nitpicky to me.

How you see yourself as a writer may or may not have been affected by teacher comments as strongly as was true for this writer. But we hope you were able to recall memories of your early writing and how you reacted to it.

If, after you have finished these exercises, you feel that there is much more in your memory that you have not yet explored, continue to write in your notebook until you believe your memories are somewhat complete. Although it might seem as if you have just taken a step backwards, you have just made an important move that will allow you to develop a new vision of yourself as a writer, as you will see later in the book.

Your Present as a Writer

Before we begin to make some suggestions about how your writing process can become more effective, we would like for you to examine what your writing is like right now. What follows is a series of questions about your writing process. Read these questions over and determine your answers to them.

1. Do you like to write at all?
2. What kinds of writing do you prefer?
3. What kinds of subjects do you find it difficult to write about?
4. What do you do before you begin to write?
5. Do you use an outline?
6. How long do you think about a topic before you begin to write?
7. How do you organize your ideas or data?
8. What kind of difficulties do you tend to get into?
9. What kind of writer's blocks do you experience?
10. What kind of environment do you prefer to write in? For example, do you like to write at a desk, or would you prefer to write while lying in bed?
11. What kind of writing rituals do you follow? Do you have to sharpen pencils before you begin? listen to music? take a bath? or wear a certain kind of clothing?
12. What are your rough drafts like?
13. How many drafts do you like to write?
14. Do you develop your best ideas when alone or when talking with someone?

15. Are your ideas clear before you start to write? Or do they become clear as you write?
16. What kind of feedback helps you to revise better?
17. When you revise your drafts, what do you tend to change?
18. When you revise, do you tend to expand or cut your rough draft?
19. What are your strengths as a writer?
20. What are your weaknesses as a writer?
21. What are some of your best experiences as a writer?
22. What are some of your worst experiences as a writer?

The responses of two very different types of writers follow. You might want to compare your answers to theirs.

Writer Number One

1. *Writing is a real pain.*

2. *If I have to write, it's better when it's about what I know about a subject—facts and information. But I'd really rather tell you about it face to face.*

3. *I have trouble with "compare and contrast" essays.*

4. *Before I write, I get all the materials together—note cards, books, thesaurus, dictionary, sharpened pencils, pad of paper, coffee pot.*

5. *I always write an outline. How else can you know what comes next?*

6. *I only think about a topic long enough to know what I'm going to write about. Then I've got to get the ideas out of my head and tell somebody.*

7. *If I can talk to a colleague, the ideas start to take shape and get organized. Then I outline.*

8. *I have a problem when there's no choice about a deadline and there's not enough time to get organized.*

9. *I have problems when there's no one around to talk out ideas with.*

10. I always write at a big table with all the necessary resources within arm's reach.

11. I never write on an empty stomach or without a good supply of caffeine ready. Also, I never start until everything needed is on the table in front of me.

12. I prefer a first draft to be not very rough, but to be a solid product. If there was a way to do it all in one sitting, that would be best. Revising is a struggle.

13. I only write one draft, if I can get away with it (I rarely can).

14. I definitely get my best ideas from talking with someone.

15. I prefer my ideas to be clear before I write.

16. The best feedback needs to be clear and to the point and give specific suggestions on rewording.

17. When I revise, I change mechanics (sentence structure, verb tense) because words don't come easily on the page. (They come a lot easier when I speak them.)

18. Teachers always told me to say more, to elaborate. I have trouble doing that unless they ask direct questions.

19. Usually I'm pretty precise and logical. My points are usually clear.

20. I often can't find the right words to write about what's on my mind. I can do it in conversation, but not on the page.

21. I like to write the annual report for the boss—there's plenty of time to plan the schedule in advance, all the necessary data are in the files, and there's a format to follow (last year's report).

22. Once the boss gave me only five days to write a proposal for a new program. He never explained clearly what he wanted or why he wanted it. It was awful.

Writer Number Two

1. I love to write.

2. I like to write about anything dealing with people and their complexities or with different ways of looking at life.

3. It's always hard to write about things I don't care about, for example, a formal analysis of some mechanical theory of how recycling widgets might shift the cost/benefit balance of industrial waste.

4. I put my feet on the desk and stare at a blank wall, and then I imagine where the piece is going.

5. I usually scribble notes on a notepad and then draw arrows from one set of scribbles to another to connect themes instead of using a formal outline.

6. I think about a topic for days, weeks, even months. The topic percolates in my unconscious mind a long time.

7. My ideas don't ever really get "organized" till after I've written a rough draft. I then rearrange sentences and paragraphs.

8. I usually get into trouble when I've overcommitted to too many things and they're all due at the same time.

9. I get blocked when I have to narrow my topic too soon— before I've had a chance to consider all the possibilities.

10. I like to write almost anywhere—I scribble whole drafts on the backs of envelopes on the subway. Sometimes I rewrite a first draft lying down on the floor. I prefer quiet environments, but if I'm really involved with my topic, I can shut out almost any sounds.

11. Rituals aren't that important. I can write or rewrite in my head almost anywhere—while gardening or mowing the lawn.

12. My rough drafts are illegible—lots of crossing out and arrows everywhere. They're also very long!

13. I expect many drafts, whether I like it or not. At minimum, I have 3 to 4 rewrites, often many more. I can never leave my work alone, even after I've submitted it!

14. I work best alone at first, then I talk with someone, then I go back to writing alone. The serious work is always done alone, however.

15. Things get clear after I write, while revising.

16. I need to know if I've made a connection with my readers, if there's at least a kernel of a neat idea that they were inspired by or led them to want to read more. If so, I can handle just about any criticism.

17. In revising, I think of emphasis and deemphasis—what words need to be added or deleted to capture the reader's fancy.

18. I always have to shorten my drafts. I have to cut out words, phrases, sentences, even whole sections. I'm very wordy.

19. I'm original. I have a flair for inspiration and for providing a new twist on things.

20. I ramble, overstate things, and sometimes get too passionate about what I'm stating.

21. I was really excited once when my colleagues said the article I wrote really helped them to understand their typical approach to work.

22. The boss made us write a rationale for how we spend our time, itemizing and categorizing each hour over the last month. I just about died when he asked us to do that.

As you can already see, every writer brings a unique set of strengths and limitations to every writing task. Some of the differences between Writer One and Writer Two are probably related to differences in personality type, as we will show later. Other differences are related to their personal history as writers. Whatever the case, it is important that each writer understand what works best for him or her. That is the point of the book.

What We Write Versus How We Write

Even confident writers sometimes try to figure out what their final sentence of a ten-page paper will be while they are composing their second or maybe third sentence. They may even worry about criticism while in the midst of struggling with the wording of a particular sentence.

Perhaps because most of us first began to write in school, we tend to think of our writing in terms of a finished product. Herbert Kohl makes this point clearly in his book *The Open Classroom:*

> In school, teachers have a tendency to consider all the work of a student on the same level. Everything a student does is supposed to be a finished product. There is little allowance for hesitant beginnings, false starts, bad ideas, impossible dreams—all the explorations writers attempt before finding their own voices and the forms appropriate to expressing them.

No matter what kinds of schools or teachers you have had, you have *right now* at your disposal a broad repertoire of ways to go about writing that can work well for you. The purpose of this book is to help you discover what those ways are.

Try to focus for a while on the process or series of different possible processes involved in writing rather than on the products of your writing.

Writing Products	Writing Processes
What we write	*How* we go about writing
What we are required to write	How we are taught to write
Mechanics: grammar, spelling	Getting motivated
Clear words	Imagining audiences
Beginnings, middles, ends	Connecting sections to one another

A shift in focus from what we write to how we write allows us to break the writing process into a series of different steps. These may include the following:

- *Prewriting:* all those things you need to do in getting ready to develop a first draft, such as doodling, going for a walk, brainstorming possible topics with a friend, jotting down ideas on a notepad, or outlining a tentative structure for your paper

- *Writing:* putting words on paper in a first attempt to get your ideas together in the form of sentences or paragraphs
- *Rewriting:* revising, editing, juggling the order of your paragraphs, deleting entire sections that don't work well, correcting errors in spelling, punctuation, and grammar

While these stages overlap, writers may have trouble when they try to focus on all of these steps at once. If you are one of those, for example, who worries too much about your reader's possible criticisms before you take pen to paper, you are focusing on *rewriting* too early. You need instead to concentrate simply on *writing*, or even on *prewriting*.

As you go through this book, you will discover that there is not just one writing process, but many. Some processes will feel comfortable to you; others will feel forced or alien. We intend to help you to find the process that comes most naturally to you.

Your Voice as a Writer

Good singers not only get the notes and words of a song right, they also express themselves in a unique style, blending sounds and lyrics with musical expressiveness. Hours of practice and hard work may have preceded their performance. But their product, at its best, will sound effortless.

Confident writers similarly have a unique voice. What they write is comfortably assisted by the way they go about writing it. Unlike music, however, there is rarely a single performance in front of an audience. A writer's voice can be crafted and adjusted during the writing process.

Return now to your answers to the twenty-two questions posed at the beginning of this chapter. Most of these questions were designed to give you an idea of the writing processes you tend to use in an effort to help you discover *how* you write. The two examples we presented not only illustrate different ways of going about writing, they also suggest how different types of people view themselves as writers. Their personalities color their approach to writing. The next chapters will explain how different writing processes can fit comfortably with certain personality types. We will go on to suggest how the style of writing you produce can best reflect the type of person you are: your special voice as a writer.

Our most important point is that *you already have ways to write that can work well for you.* If you have had difficulty with writing, our guess is that you may not have trusted your preferred ways. We have heard many writers say that they used what they called "shortcuts" to get their writing started, but always felt guilty, as if they were cheating. We believe there is no way to cheat in the process of writing. If it works for you, you should use it.

PART II

Writing Through Personality

▬◇ We now ask you to turn your attention to who you are as a person and to notice how aspects of your personality might influence how you go about writing. At this point, some readers may initially feel either anxious or skeptical about how their personality relates to their writing. Our purpose is not to uncover hidden conflicts or unresolved neuroses. Instead, we have discovered that within each person there resides the potential for strengths and gifts as a writer. The starting process may be different for different types of personalities. The nature of the writing products are also likely to vary. But the virtues of all types of writers, as of all types of people, are undeniable. The five chapters in part 2 of the book are intended to show how this can be true.

Your Preferred
Way of Writing

Think over your years of writing instruction. What are the two or three things that you remember most from your writing teachers?

It is sad that many of us remember very little from all those years of writing instruction, all the hours that we spent in English classes listening to someone try to describe the correct way to go about writing. But there is one bit of instruction that most people remember, occasionally with appreciation, frequently with dismay: the lecture on outlining. Compare your memories of outlining with the various responses that follow:

- *Boy, was it painful. Having to listen to the teacher talk about roman numerals and Arabic numbers, capital letters and lowercase letters, indenting, and watching margins was bad enough. But then having to follow these complicated instructions and actually integrate this procedure into my writing process just made things worse.*

- *Actually, some of it was pretty helpful. Through outlining, I learned to make things clear. My thoughts got organized when I outlined them. Then I felt more confident about writing.*

- *I didn't mind the idea of outlining. But I wish the teacher would have just allowed us to jot down a few basic ideas and then begin a draft. I just didn't want to write the kind of outline the teacher wanted to see. That seemed like a waste of time.*

- *I didn't like the idea of an outline at all. How could I tell the teacher what I was going to say before I said it? Eventually, I found a way to fool the teacher. I went ahead and wrote the essay, then I outlined what I had already written. What a brilliant ploy! That gave me an outline that actually related to my essay. Whenever I tried to*

*outline the essay first and then write it, I never stuck to the
outline. Too boring. I wound up with an outline and an essay that
seemed to have been written by two different people.*

As you were reading the different reactions to instruction about outlining, you were probably able to relate to one of them. Maybe you were the kind of student who liked composing formal outlines, or maybe you didn't mind outlining but just wanted to do it your way, or maybe you found the very idea of outlining ridiculous.

Outlining is only one example of writing instruction. But we could describe similar scenarios for almost all the advice that teachers give their students, or that bosses give their employees, or that self-help books give troubled writers.

When people give advice and say explicitly or implicitly that "this is what all good writers do," they may be doing more harm than good. It is not just that the advice will not work for some people. Such advice can be damaging when writers who do not follow it begin to feel that they are not good writers. Those resourceful people who figured out that the only way they could write outlines was to draft the essay first often feel that they were cheating or doing something they weren't supposed to do.

In this book, we will encourage you to believe that there is only one piece of advice that will work for all writers: Find a way that works for you. As a result of being the type of person you are, you already have ways to write that can work. You simply may have neglected them.

You might be saying to yourself, OK, that sounds nice. It gives me the freedom to avoid outlines, if I want. But doesn't this leave me without any advice at all? Isn't freedom just another word for being totally lost?

Not really. We will provide in this book a great deal of advice, but we will also suggest that each piece of advice might work for some people but not others. First, we will ask you to come to an understanding of your basic personality. Once you understand your personality type, you can begin to understand how certain kinds of advice work for some people and not others. Most importantly, you can begin to understand what works best for you and why.

Understanding Your Personality Type

In order to become aware of different sides of your personality, we will ask you to do a simple exercise: Sign your name in two different ways. The first time, simply sign your name as you would if you were signing a check or a letter. Here's how we do it:

Now do exactly the same thing right underneath your first signature, but this time sign your name with your other hand. Here's the result of our efforts:

Think about how it felt signing your name each time. The first time, when you used your preferred hand, you probably signed your name effortlessly, without even thinking about it. The second time, when you used your other hand, you probably experienced much more difficulty. Using your unpreferred hand probably took longer and required more concentration. It might also have felt awkward—like you were back in kindergarten again.

It is important to note that, barring physical disability, all people are capable of using either hand to sign their names. With practice, they might even learn to use the unpreferred hand about as reliably as the preferred one, maybe even without feeling awkward. But no training, practice, or instruction can lead people to prefer their second hand. The preference is deeply ingrained.

Our personalities can be described as having preferences that are just as habitual—maybe even innate. In the section that follows, we will be looking at four distinct aspects of personality, each of which, like handedness, has two sides. Both sides are valuable. However, one tends to lead, and the other tends to follow.

Carl Jung and the Myers-Briggs Type Indicator® Personality Inventory

The way of looking at personality differences used in this book comes mainly from the work of three people: Isabel Briggs Myers, her mother Katharine Briggs, and the Swiss psychologist Carl Jung, who inspired both Myers and Briggs. Originally, Myers and her mother became interested in personality differences because they wanted to understand how husbands and wives selected their partners. Briggs' first descriptions of personality types, written back in the early 1920s, were very similar to those Jung presented at the same time in Switzerland.

Because his system was more fully developed, Myers and Briggs soon adopted Jung's terminology and corresponded with him over the years. They later decided to design a questionnaire based on this system to help people understand themselves and others. This personality inventory was called the *Myers-Briggs Type Indicator®* (MBTI®) personality inventory. In the last fifteen years or so, the MBTI personality inventory has become the most widely used assessment instrument for working with normally functioning individuals.

As we begin to explain the kind of differences that the MBTI personality inventory acknowledges, we will discuss four different aspects or dimensions of your personality and two different ways of dealing with these aspects—each of which is like being right-handed or left-handed.

Process	Preference
How you focus your energy and attention	Extraversion (E) or Introversion (I)
How you gather information	Sensing (S) or Intuition (N)
How you make decisions	Thinking (T) or Feeling (F)
How you approach the outer world	Judging (J) or Perceiving (P)

As we describe each of these personality aspects, think about which of the two choices is most like the first hand you used to sign your name. In other words, which of the two approaches seems to come most naturally? The alternative approach will be like your unpreferred hand. You will use it, but less often and less well. If at the end of this chapter you are still uncertain about your preference, don't worry. We will discuss these concepts in much more detail in the chapters that follow. Although the descriptions in this book will give you a clear picture of each of the personality types developed by Jung, Briggs, and Myers, the most valid method for discovering your own type is to have the MBTI personality inventory administered and interpreted for you by a qualified administrator. The inventory is readily available from most counselors.

How You Focus Your Energy and Attention:
Extraversion (E) and Introversion (I)

You focus your energy in two directions: either outside yourself through Extraversion or inside yourself through Introversion. Note, however, that Extraverts are not necessarily the life of a party, and Introverts are not necessarily shy or withdrawn. Whether they like parties or not, Extraverts are the type who prefer to approach people or things by getting actively involved with them. Introverts prefer instead to pause before they speak or act. The pause gives them time to collect their thoughts, anticipate the direction they will take, and look before leaping.

Extraverts, because of their outward orientation, usually write best when thinking out loud and talking to other people, inviting them to interrupt so that a dialogue develops. They often prefer to leap into an activity with little planning and use trial and error to solve whatever problems might arise. This is why they often prefer to write an essay first and then make an outline. Extraverts tend to develop their best ideas while in the act of writing. As one Extraverted student wrote: "I never start out with a set of ideas to develop, they come as I write." Another Extraverted student wrote, "Sometimes I wonder what I am thinking when I write papers. Maybe I just write what's in my head without even thinking how it is going to sound."

Extraverts become energized by engaging the outer world actively; after a hard day's work, they may even recharge their batteries through physical exercise or meeting some friends or colleagues for conversation. They tend to find sitting in isolation emotionally and physically draining.

Because they think as they act, when in the process of putting words on paper or screen, Extraverts sometimes write sentences that ramble on, as they continue to add thought after thought. Reba, a freshman writer, explained it in this way: "As for my sentences being 'rambling,' sometimes I get more than one idea in my head and become sidetracked.... Also, it is very hard to complete a thought in a sentence because it is coming from your mind, which is just like you were talking."

Introverts usually write best when they can think alone without distractions. They may be reluctant to seek advice or feedback from others, which distracts them and interrupts their writing process. When they do receive feedback from others, they may need some time alone to let it all sink in. Introverts, in contrast to Extraverts, are more likely to recharge themselves by being alone.

When asked to add personal examples to her essay, Karen, an Introvert, wrote: "I can't think of any personal examples; I don't have that much experience." Indeed, Introverts often have very rich inner lives, but less outer experience than Extraverts to draw upon when writing personal essays.

How You Gather Information:
Sensing (S) and Intuition (N)

We find out about the world either through using our five senses—seeing, hearing, touching, smelling, and tasting—or through trusting our sixth sense—hunches or impressions. The first is a more deliberate process of gathering information. Sensing types prefer this method and are more observant of what actually exists in the world. Intuitives, on the other hand, notice possibilities. They look into the future rather than at what is in the here and now. They like to be inspired by new ways of looking at things. They may not get their facts straight all the time, but they bring an original perspective to life. They see the big picture and the abstract meaning behind what they observe.

Sensing types write best when they start with the pieces of information they know for certain; they have difficulty with beginning to write or even trusting their ideas before they grasp the facts. Indeed, for Sensing types, the visual, tangible, factual aspects of writing—accuracy, descriptive details, neatness, nice handwriting, fonts that are pleasing to the eye, good grammar—are indicators of good writing. Young Sensing types may have trouble understanding why a neat essay with no errors does not always earn a good grade. Sensing types, who need clear directions in order to do their best writing, often become frustrated by the general directions given to them by teachers or bosses. Robert, a freshman Sensing type, wrote to his teacher: "I need to find out what you expect in a paper so that I can write accordingly. Once I find out what you expect, I'm sure that my grades will be better." For Sensing types like Robert, the concrete reality of the teacher's directions give them solid grounding. Abstractions and generalities have little use for them unless they can be made practical.

Intuitives, on the other hand, begin with ideas and may pay little attention to the facts. For Intuitives, good writing is often equated with originality. Kelly, a freshman writer, speaks for many Intuitive types when she writes of the importance of originality: "Writing is like getting dressed in the way that you have a subject that needs to be dressed. You sometimes try different accessories." Intuitive types like Kelly find explicit instructions too restrictive. They often will overlook the concrete requirements of an assignment, but will become inspired by a fresh new approach to a topic.

How You Make Decisions:
Thinking (T) and Feeling (F)

When it is time to make a decision, Thinking types prefer to be objective. Feeling types, instead, prefer to concentrate on the special needs of the individuals involved. Please note that we are not talking about thinking clearly versus being emotional. Both types have emotions and both think clearly. But when an important decision is being made,

Thinking types establish a criterion, look at the pros and cons, or apply a philosophical principle. Feeling types may make the decision that is exactly right for the situation, but they may have difficulty finding the right words to explain their choice. They are more concerned with harmony, establishing and maintaining relationships with others, and following their heart, even if it conflicts with what their head says is right.

As writers, Thinking types tend to focus on the content of their message. They often believe that if they say something clearly, others will listen to them. They may, at times, fail to make their writing as engaging as it could be; their writing may even come across as being harsh or too curt. While Thinking types write better when they are experts on a topic, they don't seem to need to be as emotionally invested in it. Adrian, a Thinking type, wrote to her teacher, "My strength as a writer is that I can write on any topic."

Feeling types, in contrast, might find it difficult to write on a topic that they cannot emotionally connect with. They tend to focus on how the message is affecting their audience. Feeling types often search for just the right word, the word that they hope will capture the reader's attention. When asked about his strengths as a writer, Charles, a Feeling type, wrote the following: "I like to write and I like to put a part of myself into the things I write. I think the readers realize this, and it makes them enjoy what they are reading." Like many Feeling types, Charles is very concerned about putting himself into his writing and making contact with his audience. Feeling types are also concerned about not offending their audience, and they may even soften a message to the point that it becomes unclear.

How You Approach the Outer World:
Judging (J) and Perceiving (P)

It is not just Extraverts who approach the outer world. Introverts, too, leave the privacy of their quiet thoughts to go out into the public arena—they occasionally get on the stage, join a discussion at school, or interact with colleagues at work. This fourth dimension of personality helps both Extraverts and Introverts to understand how they approach the world around them.

Judging types like to take charge of the outer world in a planful and orderly way. Their purpose is to structure their lives so things get done. They like being decisive. In contrast, Perceiving types prefer to leave the world around them as unstructured as possible. They are inquisitive, curious, and spontaneous, and they like to take in as much information as possible before they make a decision.

When they begin a writing task, Judging types are more likely to make a plan, whether on paper or in their minds, of how they will complete it. They may limit the project so that it is more manageable, reduce their commitments to other jobs, and start writing long before the deadline nears. They tend to stick to their plan until the project is complete. They may, however, sometimes fail to reassess their plans, sticking to an ineffective strategy too long. While they often have difficulty being spontaneous, Judging types can learn, as one writer told us, to "plan to be spontaneous."

Perceiving types, on the other hand, think more about how to cover all the possible angles on the topic. They want to research the topic as much as possible before they begin to write, and they usually only begin to write when they are very close to the deadline, sometimes even the night before. Perceiving types often tell us, "I write best under pressure." They seem to need to be close to the deadline to come to closure and get ideas onto paper.

In the next four chapters, we will discuss these differences in personality and writing processes in more detail. So, if you are confused, bear with us. But we hope that you are beginning to have some idea of what your preferences might be on the four dimensions of the MBTI personality inventory. If you wish to read further about this topic, refer to the bibliography for some of the more popular books on personality type.

Getting Started:
Extraversion and
Introversion

Getting started is often the most difficult part of writing. This is especially true when we take other people's advice about how to go about writing rather than trusting our own natural way. To illustrate, we'd like to give you a flavor for different ways people focus their energy and attention when beginning to write.

Wherever you happen to be as you begin reading this chapter, we'd like you to make some adjustments to the environment around you. Try the two different exercises for getting started that follow. If you find that you are not very satisfied with the changes we suggest in the first exercise, then skip to the second one and try those recommendations instead.

Getting Started: Exercise 1

Before starting the exercises, have available an audiocassette tape recorder. While reading the exercise, walk with this book in your hand into a room where other people are present. Tell them you'd like to talk about the best way for you to get started writing. You're also seeking their reaction, in part to help you clarify your ideas.

Instead of sitting down, walk back and forth across the room as you talk. If it helps, turn on some music in the background. Read aloud to your partners a section or two from this chapter, and then interrupt your reading to share your perspective on it. You may even want to invite them to share theirs. Your goal is to get your ideas clear about what kinds of physical conditions make it easier for you to get started with a writing project. When they present an idea, don't let more than a sentence go by without jumping in with your reaction to it. Let their talk stimulate yours.

After a few minutes of throwing out thoughts, set up the tape recorder where your voice and theirs can fairly easily be recorded. Don't let this activity interfere with your continuing conversation. Turn on the recorder as soon as you have it set up.

At this point, ask your partners to help you summarize the most important conditions you need in your physical environment to get started writing. As they speak, repeat what they state in your own words into the recorder, adjusting their emphasis if it doesn't quite match what you really think is important.

What you have just begun is a process that comes naturally to Extraverted (E) writers. Extraversion means, literally, "outward turning," and Extraverts do their best thinking while interacting with people or things—even banging the keys of their computer can help them think. They best know what's on their mind once they've heard the words come out of their mouth. They learn well through trial and error, leaping into a task to find out how it works by doing it, or at least by talking about it. The more stimulation they have from the world around them, the better. A quiet corner of a library can drain their energy rather than recharge it. They may want to dictate their first drafts to someone else or speak them into a recorder.

Extraverts usually do not mind if others walk in on them while they are generating ideas. It is frankly easier to get started when their energy is stimulated by activity. Only later in a writing project is it important for them to shut out distractions.

The poet and novelist Jay Parini tells about how he and others do their best writing in restaurants. His examples sound like the words of Extraverts:

> The Left Bank of Paris was always a favorite spot for writers such as Hemingway and Sartre, both of whom seemed to thrive in the noisy atmosphere of cafes.... When I took my first teaching job at Dartmouth...I fitted out the study with a big oak desk, a typing table, a glass-fronted bookcase, filing cabinets, a telephone. Then I sat down to

work. But I couldn't. It was just too damn quiet. So I wandered downtown a few blocks where I discovered a restaurant called Lou's.... What I liked about Lou's was the distant clatter of dishes, the purr of conversation, and the occasional interruption of a friend.... Noses are blown. People cough. You feel connected.

Writing in a busy environment with lots of activity around him seemed to stimulate Parini's creative process.

Getting Started: Exercise 2

In this section, we want you to be in a place that is as quiet and solitary as possible. If you are not in such a place, go into a room where no other people are around. Close the door and lock it. If people are likely to pass by the door and want to come in, either ask them in advance not to, or put a Do Not Disturb sign on the door. If there is a phone in the room, disconnect it. Shut off any radios or televisions. If you hear noise or talking outside the room, look for a quieter place. Make sure that you have a pencil or pen and some paper with you.

As you read the rest of this section, pause every few sentences or so to stare off into space, perhaps at a blank wall. Think about what you just read and how it relates to the ways you prefer to go about completing tasks. Think perhaps about a recent project you worked on, or one you soon will deal with. When your mind clears, return to the page where you left off, reread enough to get back into the flow of the text, and then continue reading ahead.

At some point along the way, jot down on paper a few thoughts about how you like to go about working on a task: Do you prefer to work alone, with one or two others, or with as many people as possible? Do you like to plan it out first or just dive in? Don't write full sentences at first unless they come easily to you. Just doodle, even if it means drawing pictures, designs, or other figures on the page. You may find yourself pausing to stare off into space as you jot things down. After a minute or two, return to the place in this chapter where you left off, and continue reading.

This part of the exercise is very similar to what Introverts (I) do naturally. Introversion means "inward turning." When Introverts go about writing, they reflect first, anticipate what they have to say before saying it, and rehearse what they'll write before picking up a pen. They like to pause in order to gather their thoughts. Most importantly, they do not work well unless they can have a stretch of time without interruptions. They think best with quiet for concentration.

Introverts are not necessarily shy, nor does their quietness mean they are anxious, bored, or uninvolved. Their energy is simply directed inward, so it is hard for many people, especially Extraverts, to tell what's going on with them. It is wise to give Introverts a bit of advance notice, even just a few seconds, before expecting them to act or to tell you what's on their minds. They may appear hesitant while they're thinking quietly, but they prefer to pause to consider before leaping. In fact, they may only share their best thoughts the next time they see you, which gives them more time to reflect on what you asked them.

Author Annie Dillard, in *The Writing Life*, reflected an Introverted writing process:

> Appealing workplaces are to be avoided. One wants a room with no view, so imagination can meet memory in the dark....
>
> It was the Fourth of July, and I had forgotten all of wide space and all of historical time. I opened the blinds a crack like eyelids, and it all came exploding in on me at once—oh yes, the world....
>
> Write about winter in the summer. Describe Norway as Ibsen did, from a desk in Italy....

Rather than a busy environment, Dillard needs solitude to nurture her thought process.

Your Preferred Writing Process: Extraverted or Introverted?

While there are almost twice as many Extraverts in American society as Introverts, writing teachers are more often Introverted, especially at the college level. They may thus encourage students to write using an Introverted process. Both teachers and students alike need to remember that all writers, no matter where they write, must find their own way of harnessing their energy. Below is a summary of some characteristics of the preferred writing processes of Extraverted and Introverted types.

Extraversion: Active Writers	Introversion: Reflective Writers
Leap into writing	Think before writing
Outline after first draft, if at all	Outline or jot down ideas prior to first draft
Write from lived experience	Write from inner reflection
Talk out ideas before writing	Write ideas before talking
Take breaks for outer stimulation	Pause to think ahead

Extraverts need to leap into writing without forethought, to dash off a first draft as quickly as they can, to talk out their ideas where possible, and to connect what they are writing about to the experience they have lived and breathed themselves. If an outline is required, it is often best for Extraverts to prepare one after their first draft; they can then sort through what they've written (or spoken) to find what's most useful for the second draft. Breaks and interruptions along the way are helpful to them, especially if they've been writing alone for long. These breaks are not blocks, but ways to recharge their battery.

Freewriting is especially helpful to Extraverts. This is basically an active way to get words—any words—on paper and "out of their heads," as Extraverts describe it. (They can do more with their thoughts when they are outside than when they are inside.) Freewriting works like this:

> Write without a plan about anything that comes to your mind
> without editing or revising including the option of writing simply

about the difficulty you're having with writing itself and not worrying about how it's coming across very much like the way this sentence is being composed.

Because Introverts are "inward turners," they need to anticipate the direction of their writing before putting words to paper. An outline, but not necessarily a formal one, can help them sort out some ideas in advance. Quiet for concentration is essential. Interruptions by others break into thought patterns that are hard for them to retrieve. Introverts are prone to tuning others out when an important task faces them. Pauses while writing are not necessarily blocks—Introverts use these pauses to clear their minds of distracting thoughts, rework ideas they've just written, or anticipate where they're going next in the writing.

Reflections of Writers on the Writing Process: Extraversion and Introversion

The writing process of famous authors also can demonstrate aspects of their personalities. In this concluding section to the chapter, quotations from noted writers illustrate Extraverted and Introverted approaches to composition.

Biographer William Manchester described Winston Churchill's Extraverted writing process as follows:

> [Churchill] seldom puts a word on paper himself.... The humblest correspondent receives a reply, but the secretary writes it.... Once at 3:00 A.M. Winston uncharacteristically opened a window. Immediately a bat entered. The young woman on duty, more frightened of her employer than of this new uninvited immigrant...closed her eyes and kept taking down words while Churchill pursued the bat with a poker, drove it back out, and slammed the window shut—meantime not missing a phrase.

Charles Bukowski's writing process sounds similar to that of Introverts:

> There is only one place to write and that is *alone* at a typewriter. The writer who has to go *into* the streets is a writer who does not know the streets...*when you leave your typewriter you leave your machine gun and the rats come pouring through.*

Ernest Hemingway's natural Extraversion was reflected in the way he often wrote novels, described by one reviewer in the following way:

> The source of his material and spring to his imagination was his own life.... By and large he worked from life on a very short lead time. He wrote *The Sun Also Rises* while still seeing many of the people in Paris on whom he modeled its characters.... By the time of the civil war in Spain he was making trips there knowing he was collecting the people, incidents and locales for *For Whom the Bell Tolls,* a novel he completed in 1939, within months of the war's end.

Nora Ephron, author of *Heartburn* among other novels, describes the following rather Extraverted way she revises her work:

> I approach a transition by completely retyping the opening of the article leading up to it in the hope that the ferocious speed of my typing will somehow catapult me into the next section of the piece.

The following comment by novelist Vladimir Nabokov reflects an Introvert's point of view:

> I don't think the artist should bother about his audience. His best audience is the person he sees in his shaving mirror every morning. I think that the audience an artist imagines, when he imagines that kind of thing, is a room filled with people wearing his own mask.

In J. D. Salinger's *Catcher in the Rye,* Holden Caulfield was thestudent to whom classmates turned when they wanted someone to write a paper for them. Adept as he was at writing, Holden's Extraversion was reflected in the following comment:

> You don't know what interests you till you start talking
> about something that doesn't interest you most.

In *Travels With Charlie,* John Steinbeck told of his trip around America accompanied only by his dog. In that book, he wrote the following, which sounds like the words of an Introvert:

> I cannot write hot on an event. It has to ferment. I must do
> what a friend calls "mull it over."

A news release related the following typical Extraverted process about President Clinton:

> President Bill Clinton is tape-recording some of his thoughts
> about the presidency rather than writing a daily diary....
> Clinton takes notes at meetings and then—usually late at
> night—speaks into a tape recorder.

In *The Writer and Her Work,* memoirist and poet Patricia Hampl has an essay telling about the influence of family on her earliest writing:

> My Czech grandmother hated to see me with a book. She
> snatched it away if I sat still too long (dead to her), absorbed
> in my reading.... My first commissioned work was to write
> letters for her.... She dictated her letters as if she were paying
> by the word.

In addition to generation and culture, this grandmother (E) and grand-daughter (I) seem to differ in personality type.

Novelist John Updike was interviewed on a visit to a midwestern campus a few years ago. His following comments reflect a perspective on writing common to Introverts:

> I wrote my last novel in longhand, in pencil. A word proces-
> sor essentially puts two people in the room. You are staring
> at this buzzing, humming, expectant face.... It comes be-
> tween you and the words.

When asked about his relationship with other contemporary writers, he said:

> There is a common bond—we all have sat in front of a typewriter for hours, waiting for something to happen.... But in the end you are alone. Too much awareness of the literary community is not helpful. A little literary companionship goes a far distance.

Knowing What to Say: Sensing and Intuition

In order to discover how Sensing and Intuition affect your writing, we want you to write a short paragraph on a common topic that people usually find easy to write about. No one except you will have to see this paragraph. Simply put on paper some ideas without worrying about how they're coming across. Only a few sentences, or no more than a half page, will do.

In whatever way comes most naturally to you, write a short paragraph on the following topic: "A Spring Day."

You may have felt twinges of anxiety during the writing that reminded you of required assignments in some English composition class. Or you may have had fun with the exercise. Either way, your paragraph can help you see how Sensing and Intuition are used differently to contribute to the process of knowing or finding out what you have to say while writing.

Please note that in this chapter we will *not* focus so much on *what* you say while writing as on how you go about *discovering or knowing* what you want to say. What you say is a part of the finished product. Knowing or finding out what you will say is a part of your writing process.

Sensing (S) and Intuition (N) are two different ways of taking in information and finding out about things. They also affect the ways we report what we have found out. We all use both every day, but one comes a bit more naturally to some of us, with the other following.

The Sensing (S) Approach to Writing

Read over your paragraph, and compare it to two paragraphs written by other individuals who completed the same exercise. The first was written by a Sensing type:

> *Spring is the season that follows winter and comes before summer. The temperature becomes warmer and the leaves come out on the trees. It's the time that I switch the clothes in my closets, do a general cleaning, paint, and prepare the garden for planting.*

What is most noticeable about this person's paragraph is that she reports real, factual information. Every statement in this paragraph is verifiable:

- We can observe that spring follows winter and comes before summer.
- We have thermometers to testify that it is warmer.
- We can see whether leaves come out on trees or not.
- A quick search into this person's closets can tell us whether she switched the clothes or not; a similar look around her house will tell whether she got around to cleaning, painting, or preparing the garden.

Sensing types usually like to rely on what their five senses tell them about the world: what they really saw, heard, touched, smelled, or tasted. These pieces of information help to place their feet on solid ground, because they've been there. Not every Sensing type will write a paragraph like the one above, of course. But the way they prefer to gather and report information does tend to include:

- *Verifiable material.* They feel more grounded when they can point directly to where their data came from.
- *Actual information.* Their observations tend to focus on concrete, tangible things.
- *Specific examples.* But they may not show how these examples fit together to create a theme.

- *A realistic and practical perspective.* What they tell about can be useful in solving a problem.

- *A sequential process.* They start at the beginning and move step-by-step through the points that have to be covered in order to reach the end.

Sensing types not only prefer to be explicit themselves, but they also want others to be this way. If they are required to write for someone else, Sensing types can become anxious unless they have clear instructions about what is expected. A precise model to follow suits them well, since it is practical and useful.

James Michener's novels, while fictional in story line, are almost always based on careful research of the history and culture of the people who populate his stories. Similar to the writing of Sensing types, his stories are also sequential. A *New York Times Book Review* description of his latest book says the following about Michener:

> If there has been any guiding principle in James A. Michener's distinguished career, it would seem to be the maxim "Write about what you know." And Mr. Michener has always gained knowledge of the world he writes about because he does his homework. His gift as a novelist is not philosophical speculation, glorious language or the creation of complex characters; rather, it is assimilating an enormous amount of data *and then* presenting the reader with the Big Picture. (italics added)

The Intuitive (N) Approach to Writing

Now let's notice how an Intuitive writer responded to the exercise on writing about a spring day.

> Spring is the time of rebirth. The earth is awakening after the long winter's sleep. The air is full of the smell of blossoming trees and bird songs. There is romance in the air after the winter's harshness; it's the mating season. A feeling of joy comes over me as I experience nature's metamorphosis.

What we notice quickly from this person's paragraph is that she writes from imagination. She may, of course, have experienced a particular spring day that led her to the impressions above. But she does not tell about the direct experience itself, as did the Sensing type. Instead, the Intuitive gives us metaphors, impressions, and an idea of what inspires her, not what she does, sees, or accomplishes. Almost nothing is verifiable, but her words are instead used as symbols:

- You may have witnessed at one time or another a birth (of a baby chick or your younger brother), but a "rebirth" is harder to verify.

- Alarm clocks can awaken us in the morning; but the process of "the earth awakening" is more fluid and hard to pin down.

- Likewise, we can see or smell blossoms, but "blossoming" is a process observed not by the five senses, but by the sixth.

- "Romance is in the air" for this writer; it may not seem very romantic at all to someone else.

- "Nature's metamorphosis" is a term that captures a *spirit,* not a *fact,* about spring days.

Teachers in classrooms around the country respond differently to paragraphs like these two. Some find the Sensing type's paragraph too factual and uninspired; they may prefer the Intuitive's paragraph instead for its fresh imagery or originality. Others find the second paragraph trite and full of clichés; these teachers often prefer the first one, with solid material from which to work: a definition, some facts, and concrete experience. Occasionally, teachers find fault with both paragraphs; they were, after all, written in only two or three minutes.

It is important, however, for us to suspend judgment on these writers, and on our own writing as well, at least for the moment. In any piece, there are potential virtues to build upon. Intuitives prefer:

- *Imagined material.* They might not show you exactly how they got their idea, but they want it to be original.

- *Conceptual symbols.* They use metaphors and indirect ways of expressing themselves.

- *General perceptions.* However, they may not remember to give specific illustrations of their big picture.

- *An impressionistic perspective.* They will give you the essence of their idea to set the tone, but leave the details to be implied.

- *A global process.* They leap into the middle of their idea and then branch out from there.

The Intuitive mind tends to think in brainstorming fashion; practical steps tend to slow it down and stifle its originality. Whereas Sensing types like to follow a path they have followed before (because it worked, or at least is familiar and therefore real), Intuitives like instead to explore paths that have never before been imagined—often just because they are different.

E.L. Doctorow was featured in an October 20, 1985, issue of the *New York Times Magazine* as "The Myth Maker." In that article, he told of Henry James' "parable about what writing is":

> He posits a situation where a young woman who has led a sheltered life walks past an army barracks, and she hears a fragment of soldiers' conversation coming through a window. And she can, if she's a novelist, then go home and write a true novel about life in the army. You see the idea? The immense, penetrative power of the imagination and the intuition.

Your Preferred Writing Process: Sensing or Intuitive?

Your paragraph on "A Spring Day" (*what* you wrote) may or may not have been like either of the two examples given. But it can be helpful to consider which of these two processes of writing (*how* you wrote) came more naturally. Below is a summary of some characteristics of the preferred writing processes of Sensing and Intuitive types.

| Sensing: | Intuitive: |
Observant Writers	Imaginative Writers
Want specific directions	Create their own directions
Start with facts	Start with original ideas
Say it simply and directly	Say it with subtlety or complexity
Report what they know	Report what they imagine
Give verifiable material	Give hypotheses and implications
Use what worked before	Try out new ways

You can (and at school or at work, you often must) use both kinds of writing. If you are blocked or very anxious about writing, try to find which is a more comfortable home base for you—like the hand you use to sign your name. Employ this process whenever you can. You will then have more energy to use the opposite process if required.

As a writer, you can use different approaches to the various elements of your text. The following examples illustrate the difference between two writers' approaches to characterization.

Popular novelist Danielle Steel uses the Sensing approach:

> I know my characters. I know where they came from, who
> their grandmothers were, how their parents treated them
> when they were little. It's the characters' history that makes
> them who they are, and my characters are very real.

Contrast the Sensing approach to that of playwright Tennessee Williams who said the following about his writing, reflecting an Intuitive's perspective:

> The critics still want me to be a poetic realist and I never
> was. All my great characters are larger than life, not realistic.
> In order to capture the quality of life in two and a half hours,
> everything has to be concentrated, intensified.

In the general American public there appear to be at least two Sensing types for every Intuitive one. In the elementary grades,

Sensing teachers especially predominate. But the higher up the academic ladder you move, the more theory and abstraction are valued, which attracts Intuitives. Sensing types would rather put what they have learned to practical use before they go on for further schooling. Myers distinguished Intuitive intelligence, which is "quickness of understanding," from Sensory intelligence, which is more often "soundness of understanding." The latter, being more practical, is often less valued in higher education.

Our preference for Sensing or Intuition profoundly affects how we go about finding out what to say while writing. Both are important; indeed good writing includes both facts and possibilities, both concepts and examples. Our personality type thus can guide us to use one process first, and to fill in with its opposite later.

Reflections of Writers on the Writing Process: Sensing and Intuition

What follows are examples of the writing processes of famous authors, some favoring Sensing, others Intuition.

Barbara Tuchman is a historian well known for *The Guns of August, The Proud Tower,* and other volumes. In describing her approach to writing history, she noted "the value of corroborative detail." Like many Sensing types, she described herself as a "disciple of the ounce versus those theoreticians of the gallon jugs." Her wry wit seems to be directed toward the Sensing–Intuition difference in historical writing in the following quotation:

> Certainly many serious thinkers write in the abstract and many people read them with interest and profit and even, I suppose, pleasure. I respect this ability, but I am unable to emulate it.

Joseph Heller, author of *Catch 22* as well as other novels, reflected an Intuitive perspective when he wrote the following:

I don't know why my imagination takes me where it does. I just feel so lucky to get a single idea for a novel that I can write about. When I get one, my ruminations and daydreaming grow and lead to other things.

Doris Lessing expresses the following view, typical of many Sensing types we know:

I've always disliked words like *inspiration*. Writing is probably like a scientist thinking about some scientific problem, or an engineer about an engineering problem.

Historical novelist Mary Renault researched ancient novels on ancient Greece by going on archeological digs, letting every vase or artifact tell what life was like in the novel's era. When asked by her biographer what she would like best to be remembered for, her answer was typical of what many Sensing types report:

As someone who got it right.

Novelist Herman Melville presented an Intuitive bias when he stated:

It is better to fail in originality than to succeed in imitation.

Deciding How
to Say It:
Thinking and Feeling

As in the last chapter, we would like you once again to write a short paragraph. You will again compare your paragraphs (and the processes used to arrive at those products) to those written by different types of people.

We have a new topic for you to write about this time. As before, write for no more than half a page, in whatever way comes most naturally to you, on the following subject: "A Christmas Tree."

Whatever you have written can be useful to show how you best make decisions about writing, especially about how to say what you want to say. Thinking (T) and Feeling (F) are two different ways we approach decision making in order to arrive at conclusions and make judgments. Thinking is more objective, while Feeling is more personal. Just as we have both hands at our disposal, we all use both Thinking and Feeling every day. But one comes more easily to us and gives us a sound foundation from which to use the other. In this chapter, we will emphasize how Thinking types and Feeling types go about making decisions on the emphasis and tone of their writing, the one type favoring an emotional distance (T), and the other type favoring personalization (F).

The following two paragraphs were both written by Sensing types. However, one is a Sensing Thinking type (ST) and the other a Sensing Feeling type (SF). While both passages are concrete, reflecting a preference for Sensing, one is more objective (ST) and the other is more personal (SF):

ST

Green, symmetrical branches with a trunk, and instead of leaves it has needles. The tree is shaped like a cone with the top part of the cone the most narrow part. It is filled with lights, ornaments, tinsel, and other decorations and is a place to put presents under at Christmas time. On top of the tree is a star. Trees cost between twenty and fifty dollars and can be procured at a store or at a "chop your own" facility. They are also a fire hazard if not watered properly. It also denotes the start of Christmas season.

SF

My Christmas tree is beautiful, bright, and cheerful. It is green and full. It has multicolored lights. It has ornaments of all different shapes and colors. I have lots of teddy bear ornaments on this tree. It stands in the corner of my living room by the window. It has brightly colored packages under it. These packages are for close friends and family.

Similar to the paragraph in the last chapter that described a spring day in concrete terms, both of these paragraphs on a Christmas tree have verifiable, tangible information in them. The examples are specific and seem to refer to actual Christmas trees that the writers have witnessed. But the first paragraph is more of an objective report, and the second one very personalized.

Thinking is a process of decision making that follows logic. Thinking types establish criteria from which they make their judgments, and they make these standards as objective as possible. Personal values get in the way of clear, tough-minded decision making, they believe.

When they write, Sensing Thinking (ST) types, like the author of the first paragraph above, prefer to give the facts straightforwardly, as in "Green, symmetrical branches...." They tend to be critical, but their criticism is based on objective evidence: "They are also a fire hazard if not watered properly."

Feeling, on the other hand, is a process of decision making that follows personal values. Feeling types decide from the heart, even if the decision appears to conflict with what reason tells them. They believe that logic alone fails to motivate people they care about. Being personally invested in a project is their goal.

When they write, Sensing Feeling (SF) types, like the author of the second paragraph above, prefer to give us the facts in a special way, expressing what's important either to them ("My Christmas tree...") or to the people they care about ("These packages are for close friends and family."). While the language of the ST writer is more analytical ("symmetrical," "shaped like a cone," "denotes the start of the Christmas season"), the SF writer uses language that expresses appreciation ("beautiful, bright, and cheerful").

We find a similar difference in the way Thinking and Feeling types use Intuition. Many times, people use the words "intuitive" and "feeling" interchangeably. In the way we're using them here, they are separate processes. Intuition, as we noted in the last chapter, is a way of taking in information, that is, through the sixth sense, impressions, hunches, and imagining. Feeling is a way of making decisions. The difference may be seen when we look next at two other "Christmas Tree" paragraphs, the first written by an Intuitive Feeling (NF) type, the second by an Intuitive Thinking (NT) type.

NF

I was raised in a Jewish family that always had Christmas trees. Among my Jewish friends I felt special because I had something they didn't. Among my Christian friends I felt more normal. We used to get live trees and then plant them in the yard. Six of them are still in the yard of the house where I grew up. As a child, Christmas trees meant lots of presents. As a mother and housewife, Christmas trees mean a lot of work. I sometimes wish my children were being raised by a mother who was raised in a Jewish family that didn't have Christmas trees.

NT

On a lonely mountainside near the tree line, there was a small pine protected by two huge boulders. Because it was protected from the wind and weather it grew to a size unmatched by the other trees around it. I first saw it when I was cross-country skiing at the age of eleven. That is my own Christmas tree, I thought, too beautiful to ever be cut down and wasted for a single season. It is still there, more beautiful than ever.

There are certainly similarities between the NF and NT paragraphs. Both writers, as Intuitives, are interested in the symbolic meaning of Christmas trees. The NF writes that "Christmas trees meant lots of presents," and the NT tells a story that makes the Christmas tree into a symbol for permanence and beauty.

There also is the expression of personal investment in both. But the NF expresses this Feeling material from start to finish—notice the emphasis on what Christmas trees meant or mean to her, and how much these feelings are tied to the people in her life. The NT, however, builds up to values and expressing personal investment with a cause-and-effect kind of reasoning: "Because it was protected from the wind and weather it grew to a size unmatched by the other trees around it." That solid foundation of objectivity then allowed the NT writer to risk the expression of subjective material: "That is my own Christmas tree." In a later chapter, we will talk more carefully about how each type develops the use of all of these processes of writing.

Behind the content of the writing of Thinking and Feeling types are very different processes. Thinking types like to follow an organizational pattern, with criteria to help them decide what to say next. Above all, they like to be clear. Feeling types write from a sense of flow, choosing a different word here or there to capture a mood, even if they can't tell you what reasons they had for those choices. They are often more concerned about appealing to their readers than the content of their message.

Your Preferred Writing Process: Thinking or Feeling?

Compare your Christmas Tree paragraph to the four presented here. Look first for whether you rely on facts and observable information, as in Sensing, or on impressions and imagined material, as in Intuition. Also, look for whether you tend to write principally in an objective, analytical Thinking way, or from the heart, subjectively, in a Feeling fashion. Both ways are useful, but one probably takes precedence for you over the other. Below are some of the characteristics of the preferred writing processes of Thinking and Feeling types.

Thinking:	Feeling:
Objective Writers	Personal Writers
Write from a distance	Write from what they value
Focus on what they're saying	Focus on how it's expressed
Seek to be clear	Seek to stimulate and motivate
Critically analyze arguments	Qualify and soften their points
Guide writing decisions by criteria	Guide writing decisions by a sense of flow
Seek organization of ideas	Personalize with human stories

It is also very important to realize the real strengths that naturally come out of your preferred style. Thinking types have a gift for clarity and directness when they learn to trust their preferred way of communicating. Feeling types have a gift for connecting with their reader and for investing personal energy in their writing.

William Styron, author of *Sophie's Choice* and *The Confessions of Nat Turner*, among other novels, likens his writing to the analytical or Thinking process of playing chess:

It's like a chess game in a curious way. I'm not a good chess player, but I'm fascinated by how there are aspects of novel writing that resemble chess: you are anticipating a multiplicity of choices, you're heading in a certain direction, so you want to make sure that your moves at this point will be symmetrical, so that when you get to point B, everything fits together.

David Lawton, Professor of Linguistics at Central Michigan University, articulated the perspective of many Thinking types in a short article about writing an essay that was published in the *Chronicle of Higher Education*:

> I think most of us could agree that an acceptable standard of good writing is the ability to produce an intellectually mature essay that is grammatically and stylistically correct and that proceeds logically from a premise supported by example and argument to a conclusion.

South American novelist Isabel Allende reflected the view of many Feeling type writers with the following:

> A book is never an end in itself, it is only a way to touch someone—a bridge extended across a space of loneliness and obscurity—and sometimes it is a way of winning other people to our causes.

American novelist F. Scott Fitzgerald's views are also similar to those of Feeling types:

> Whether it's something that happened twenty years ago or only yesterday, I must start out with an emotion—one that's close to me and that I can understand.

The problem is that society doesn't always encourage us to use our natural preferences. Instead, our teachers, our employers, or others may give us the message that there's one right kind of writing. They also imply that there's one right process to use to go about writing.

Males and females especially get stereotyped this way. In most cultures, boys and men are expected to be tough-minded and logical (Thinking). Their writing process often shows it, whether this method really suits them well or not. Girls and women are expected to be the opposite: sensitive, warm, and personally invested. They tend to learn to write in Feeling ways, whether this is their preferred way or not. But as we will show in chapter 14, we grow as writers when we first gain confidence in our natural preferences.

Reflections of Writers on the Writing Process: Thinking and Feeling

Following are several quotations from famous authors that illustrate different approaches to writing as explained by the Thinking–Feeling dimension.

Richard Selzer, author of *Mortal Lessons* and *Confessions of a Knife,* is a surgeon who has written, in very human fashion, about the personal experience of performing surgery. The Thinking–Feeling dimension seems reflected in many of his comments:

> In the operating room the patient must be anesthetized in order that he feel no pain. The surgeon too must be "anesthetized" in order to remain at some distance from the event: when he cuts the patient, his own flesh must not bleed.... Dispassion is an attribute. But the surgeon-writer is not anesthetized. He remains awake; sees everything; censors nothing.

Canadian novelist Robertson Davies has regularly drawn from Jung's ideas to inspire his work. In describing himself, he writes:

> I am not of formidable intellect.... In Jungian terms I am a feeling person with strong intuition. I *can* think, I've *had* to think, and I *do* think, but thinking isn't the first way I approach any problem.

The following quotation from Annie Dillard's *The Writing Life* reflects a Feeling point of view, that is, wanting to please others:

The impulse to keep to yourself what you have learned is not only shameful, it is destructive. Anything you do not give freely and abundantly becomes lost to you. You open your safe and find ashes.

The Russian playwright Anton Chekhov expressed the following perspective on writing, one that is common to many Thinking types:

> A writer must be as objective as a chemist: he must abandon the subjective line; he must know that dung-heaps play a very reasonable part in a landscape, and that evil passions are as inherent in life as good ones.

The problem of revising while writing initial drafts can haunt writers of all ages. In *Emily Climbs*, a children's novel by L. M. Montgomery, Emily keeps a diary, which she thinks of as "a personal friend and a safe confidant." In it, she discusses her teacher's reactions to her writing:

> Mr. Carpenter says I use far too many italics. He says it is an early Victorian obsession, and I must strive to cast it off.... I *love* reading the dictionary (Yes, those italics are *necessary*, Mr. Carpenter. An ordinary "love" wouldn't express my feelings at all!). Words are such *fas*cinating things (I caught myself at the first syllable that time!).

Martin Luther King Jr. appears to have developed his way with words over time. Stephen B. Oates, in his biography of King, seemed to suggest that King's early sermons were written in a style similar to that of a Thinking type:

> At first his sermons tended to be sober and intellectual, like a classroom lecture. But he came to understand the emotional role of the Negro church, and how much black folk needed this precious sanctuary to vent their frustrations and let themselves go.... What was good preaching if not "a mixture of emotion and intellect?"

E. B. White suggested the following advice to writers, most of it consistent with the mindset of a Thinking type:

Place yourself in the background;...work from a suitable design; do not overwrite; do not overstate; avoid the use of qualifiers; do not affect a breezy style;...do not explain too much; avoid fancy words; do not take shortcuts at the cost of clarity....

Getting It Done:
Judging and Perceiving

Suppose that you had an assignment to write a short autobiography on how you came to write in your natural way. Let's assume that a completed draft of your autobiography should be finished in ten days. Now think about how you would go about completing the project—getting it done.

Below you will find the words of two writers describing their very different methods of managing time and resources over the next ten days. Read the two options and ask yourself which one is most like the way you work best. You probably have operated both ways at different times. What you need to decide here is which way works best for you.

Getting It Done: Option One

Since I know that the writing project should be finished in ten days, I will start planning out a schedule today. First, I will spend some time thinking about the project. Can it be broken down into sections: research, thinking about the topic, first draft, revisions, final typing, and so on? If it can, then I will decide when I want to complete each section. Preferably, I will set aside a specific period of time each day to work on the task. I may even want to make daily goals, like writing one page each day. That way I know that I am staying on task and making enough progress to complete the assignment on time.

I also know that I do not live in a vacuum. There are other people in my life, other things I have to do. Because this writing assignment is a priority, I will plan how to keep other commitments from interfering with it. Some can be delayed for the ten days, but others I will schedule in. Maybe I can work on this autobiography each morning and other projects in the afternoon. I prefer to work on the most important projects, such as this one, first.

To complete an autobiography like this one on how I came to write the way I do, I'll want to decide which key points I'll cover. Then I'll look for examples for each point. Once I get just enough material collected to begin writing, I'll start. If I collect too much information directly related to the topic, it will be difficult to write.

Each day I will plan to stop at a point where I know what will come next, where it is easy to start again. That way I will not have trouble motivating myself to get started the next morning.

It is also important to schedule time for revising. My rough drafts are often fairly short, what I call "skeleton drafts"—just the basic ideas that I expand on during revision.

I usually have to get my work done before I play. Work and writing can be fun for me, but I relax more when the job is done and when the day's tasks are checked off my list.

However, I know I have a tendency to get a little carried away with sticking to schedules. I often forget that it really does help me to plan a few minutes every day to ask myself, How are things going? Do I need to change my approach? Do I need to change my schedule?

Getting It Done: Option Two

I like to keep my options open whenever I begin a writing project. I don't work well when I'm fenced in too much. I need to have fun with it. Even when serious work has to be done, I can play at any time.

Since this autobiography is due in ten days, I know that a major amount of my energy will be expended as that deadline approaches. That doesn't mean I'm procrastinating, as many people believe *(especially as my teachers used to believe!). I truly do work best with a burst of energy at the last minute.*

What I'll be doing between now and the seventh or eighth day is very important to this writing project. I'll be collecting ideas as they come to me about different topic options. I'll also want to look at all the possible angles on this topic. I will not put other projects aside (unless their deadlines are much further away), but will keep working on them along the way. I actually get interesting ideas about one project while I'm working on several others. I like to have the freedom to jump from one idea to another as they come to me. Sometimes I lose track of where I started, and my notes for one project often get lost in with those for another. But I'm clearly more motivated to work on a writing project if I can just let things develop when they develop.

When I actually start writing, I absolutely like to include in the first draft everything I can find out about the topic. For this project, maybe I'll pull out old school papers and read over teachers' comments. It might also be fun to look through old journals and diaries I kept when I was in school to see if there are any ideas about how I learned to write. I could talk to my parents, brothers and sisters, or former classmates. That way I can get some possible quotes or excerpts to build my paper around. One reason I prefer to wait until near the deadline to begin writing my first drafts is that then I know I've included all the information and perspectives I can.

I do, however, usually have trouble near the deadline because there's not enough time to condense all the material I've collected. I almost always have too much. It's very hard to let go of an interesting idea or quote. I know I have to shorten my first drafts. Otherwise, they ramble on and on. Maybe I can ask to extend the deadline so I can clean it up. On the other hand, that'll just give me more time to come up with different possibilities, and the paper might wind up even longer. Occasionally, I've been known to change my entire direction the night before a paper is due. Somehow, I always get it done. The deadline does make me anxious. But it's also kind of fun to see how much I can juggle at the last minute and still pull it off.

Your Preferred Writing Process: Judging or Perceiving?

Every writer experiences the pressure of deadlines, and many writers feel like they've procrastinated on writing projects. Judging (J) types, however, work best when they get organized early. They may feel like they've waited until the last minute, but they usually get that feeling during the last week. In contrast, Perceiving (P) types are often literally working at the last minute. They may ask for an extension of the deadline because a new piece of information or an interesting twist in their writing emerged as they neared completion. Below are some of the characteristics of the preferred writing processes of Judging and Perceiving types.

Judging:	Perceiving:
Decisive Writers	Inclusive Writers
Narrow options to decide on topic	Keep topic options open and flexible
Set and follow a schedule toward completion	Let deadlines motivate completion
Work on one project at a time	Let unfinished projects assist one another
Write short first drafts	Include everything related in first drafts

Judging is a way of dealing with the outside world that involves taking charge of it in order to get things done. Judging types like to regulate things: their schedules, the materials and resources they need, and sometimes other people (especially if they're also Extraverts). This is not necessarily for the purpose of being controlling. They simply want things settled. They will keep options open only when they have deliberately chosen to do so, with an end date firmly in mind. They prefer to decide on a writing topic early, set and follow a schedule to completion, work mainly on one project at a time, and state things conclusively without too many words.

According to his biographer, Martin Luther King Jr. prepared his sermons according to a careful schedule, similar to the way many Judging types approach writing.

> At prescribed hours during the week, he closed his office door and devoted himself to his sermon for the next Sunday. On Tuesday he would sketch an outline, on Wednesday do research and decide what illustrations and life situations to use, and on Friday and Saturday write the sermon on lined yellow pages.... Then on Sunday he would preach without notes...as though he were extemporizing.

Perceiving, on the other hand, is a way of allowing the outside world to inform us of all the curious things there are to be noticed. Decisions get made when the outer world requires that they be made. Perceiving types do take charge, but only when it's clear that decisiveness is necessary. To do so sooner is to rush to judgment. Perceiving types are likely to change their minds anyway when the delight of an unexpected idea comes to them. If they can wait until the last minute, the finished project is more likely to include more material that can relate to the topic. They would rather be inclusive than decisive. Their first drafts are therefore likely to be longer than those of Judging types because they want to cover all the bases.

There are slightly more Judging types (55%) than Perceiving types (45%) in the general U.S. population. However, among teachers and managers in organizations, who assign writing tasks to their students and employees, the percentage of Judging types often exceeds seventy-five percent. We thus tend to find more advice on good writing that favors the planful, take-charge approach of the Judging preference, as is illustrated in the number of quotations in the concluding section to this chapter.

When we come to work closely with writers, we find a fascinating paradox at work on this dimension of personality. That is, Judging types often appear to be more decided and fixed than they are. They do, indeed, like to get things settled, but they may also have an inner reservoir of adaptability that others do not see at the outset.

Especially when they plan time to attend to unexpected new pieces of information, they can very adaptable, as was shown above in the "extemporaneous" style of Martin Luther King Jr.'s sermon delivery, which followed careful planning.

Conversely, Perceiving types often appear more disoriented and unfocused that they actually are. They do, indeed, prefer to keep options open. But they may also have a subtle decisiveness to them that others are not aware of. When it is time to decide on a direction for their writing, they do in fact decide, even if only as the deadline approaches. The following quotation from Mark Twain illustrates his ability to keep many unfinished writing projects alive at once, which appears unfocused, but which came to be quite "intentional." In his autobiography, he described, in his inimitable way, his own development as a writer. His process sounds very much like that of a Perceiving type:

> There has never been a time in the past thirty-five years when my literary shipyard hadn't two or more half-finished ships on the way, neglected and baking in the sun; generally there have been three or four; at present there are five. This has an unbusiness-like look but it was not purposeless, it was intentional.... It was by accident that I found out that a book is pretty sure to get tired along about the middle and refuse to go on.... When the manuscript had lain in a pigeonhole two years I took it out one day and read the last chapter that I had written. It was then that I made the great discovery that when the tank runs dry you've only to leave it alone and it will fill up again in time, while you are asleep—also while you are at work at other things and are quite unaware that this unconscious and profitable celebration is going on.

King and Twain, both masters of the written word, employed very different approaches to their writing. The personality type qualities of Judging and Perceiving can help us to appreciate varying ways of going about getting writing projects done, the one process generally more planful from start to finish, the other more flexible, inclusive, and open to options until the project is due. Either way, the project does get done.

Reflections of Writers on the Writing Process: Judging and Perceiving

What follows are characterizations of the writing processes of other noted authors as they illustrate differences on the Judging–Perceiving dimension.

A review of Claudia Tate's book *Black Women Writers at Work* noted that within the cultural heritage of African Americans, there is a wide variety of approaches. This passage describes the differences in ways that sound like those between Judging and Perceiving types:

> ...from Maya Angelou's no-nonsense, roll-up-your-sleeves craftsmanship in autobiography to Toni Cade Bambara's mad dashes through her fiction: "I babble along, heading I think in one direction, only to discover myself tugged in another, or sometimes I'm absolutely snatched into an alley."

A central character in *The Accidental Tourist*, a novel by Anne Tyler, is an author of guidebooks for people forced to travel on business. Macon, who shows characteristics of Judging types, has a system for everything his traveling readers would face. He also has a system for his writing:

> As much as he hated the travel, he loved the writing—the virtuous delights of organizing a disorganized country, stripping away the inessential and the second-rate, classifying all that remained in neat, terse paragraphs.... He spent pleasurable hours dithering over questions of punctuation. Righteously, mercilessly, he weeded out the passive voice.

The surgeon Richard Selzer compared the process of writing with the conduct of medical practice, which tends to attract more Judging than Perceiving types, especially into the field of surgery. He wrote:

A surgical operation is rather like a short story. You make the incision, rummage around inside for a bit, then stitch up. It has a beginning, a middle and an end. If I were to choose a medical specialist to write a novel, it would be a psychiatrist. They tend to go on and on. And on.

Novelist George Orwell wrote the following, reflecting the views of many Judging types:

Never use a long word where a short one will do. If it is possible to cut a word out, always cut it out.

The French philosopher and author Voltaire is quoted as follows, consistent with the views of Judging types:

The secret of being a bore...is to tell everything.

In what sounds like the struggle of a writer with Perceiving preferences, filmwriter Woody Allen described the evolution of his scripts as follows:

Choosing an idea sometimes goes on to painful obsessional heights; you wear yourself down after weeks of getting up with one idea, then changing your mind twenty minutes later.

American poet Robert Frost was very clear in the following passage on what is required of writing, similar to the views of many Judging types:

Discipline. Tightness. Firmness. Crispness. Sternness. And sternness in our lives. Life is tons of discipline. Your first discipline is your vocabulary; then your grammar and your punctuation.

Kurt Vonnegut likens the process of writing a novel to that of making a movie in this description, portraying a Perceiving process:

> All sorts of accidental things will happen after you've set up the camera.... Something will happen at the edge of the set and perhaps you can go on with that.... You set the story in motion, and as you're watching this thing begin, all these opportunities will show up.

Scott Peck's *The Road Less Traveled* has been on the paperback bestseller list of the *New York Times* for over 600 weeks. Similar to Judging types, Peck suggests that we employ discipline and "schedule the pain and pleasure of life." In writing an early section of the book, he tells us:

> I had run into a snag.... A portion of what I had written on the subject...seemed completely unsatisfactory to me. It clearly had to be extensively enlarged in order to make meaningful the concepts I had discussed therein, yet I felt this enlargement would detract from the flow of work.

At that point, a friend's wife told him of a book she had recently read, in which Peck, upon reading it, found a solution to his dilemma:

> The next morning I condensed the section of my book to a small concise paragraph, and in a footnote referred the reader to the Wheelis book for an ideal elaboration of the subject.

A classical example of a Perceiving type pushing the limits of a writing deadline is that of Isabel Myers, author of the MBTI personality inventory, who read that a New York publisher was sponsoring a contest for the best mystery detective novel, with a deadline of January 1, 1929. She decided to give it a try. Her biographer, Frances W. Saunders, noted that

> the more Isabel wrote the more enthusiastic she became....
> By mid-December...sixteen chapters were done, with four or

five more to go. The day before Christmas, when she had only two more chapters to write, first Ann then Peter [her daughter and son] came down with the flu. To finish seemed hopeless until Paul [a family friend]…volunteered his steno-graphic services. For two solid days—December 28 and 29—Paul typed. Isabel wired [the publisher] to ask whether the manuscript was due on Monday, December 31, since January 1 was a holiday. They wired back that the due date would be January 2, a reprieve that seemed to Isabel "like an extra month." On New Year's Day, at midnight, Paul typed the last chapter; Isabel got to bed at 3:30 A.M., and Ann woke at 6:00. Leaving a sitter with the children, she was off to New York to deliver in person the finished manuscript of *Murder Yet to Come* to an unimpressed secretary.

Isabel, a Perceiving type to the core, heard the next month that her novel won the competition.

PART III

Sixteen Approaches to Writing

●◇ There are, of course, as many approaches to writing as there are writers. What we have included in this next section, however, is a description of the writing approaches of sixteen types of people. Their types result from the combination of preferences on the personality dimensions discussed in the preceding chapters.

Four letters give you a shorthand way of referring to your four preferences. Together, they stand for your personality type. For example, ISTJ indicates a person who prefers Introversion, Sensing, Thinking, and Judging.

It is important to note, however, that a "type" of person is much more than a loose collection of four preferences. Jung's theory explains in depth how people of a given type tend to develop at different points in their life cycle. It is beyond the scope of this book to describe these complex dynamics, and we refer the reader to other sources in the bibliography for this explanation. You can also refer to the appendix for a useful thumbnail sketch of how Isabel Myers described each of the sixteen personality types.

The sixteen approaches to writing are clustered into four chapters. The four type combinations discussed in each chapter have characteristics related to the middle two letters of their type formula: either ST, SF, NF, or NT. In our many years of experience with writers, we have found that these four clusters of preferences provide an especially useful way to understand different approaches to writing. It is as if each cluster identifies a general neighborhood in which a writer resides. Within that neighborhood (ST, for example), the residents share a number of writing processes in common. Also within that neighborhood reside four more specific types of writers, with special characteristics akin to their street and address. Each of these patterns represents one of the sixteen types.

The characterizations that follow result from our work with our students, colleagues, and other writers over the course of our professional careers. After we completed a draft of each description, we sent it to a number of mature writers of that type for comments, refinements, and revisions. Where possible, the actual language used by those respondents was retained in the description.

Each description begins with general characteristics of that particular personality type. What follows are statements about that type's preferred writing process, writing strengths and limitations, natural style of writing, preferred contexts for writing, and common blocks and how they best overcome them.

If you already have received a profile from the *Myers-Briggs Type Indicator®* (MBTI®) personality inventory, and you are fairly confident that the reported type is true for you, then your reading of the writing approach for that type is likely to be most helpful. If you have not completed the MBTI, you will still find useful the description fitting the best guess of your type from reading the preceding chapters. In either case, you will also benefit from reading how writers of many different types approach their work, and you may pick up some useful ideas from their way of doing things. At the very least, you will probably understand how different the writing processes of individuals can be.

Four Sensing Thinking Approaches to Writing

The four types of writers described in this chapter all share common preferences for Sensing (S) and Thinking (T). These writers tend to take a no-nonsense approach to life. They find out about the world through the verifiable processes of direct observation and the five senses (S), and they arrive at a carefully constructed conclusion that can be explained with logic and evidence (T). Isabel Myers, in her classic book on psychological type, *Gifts Differing,* described these individuals as "practical and matter-of-fact types."

ST writers often view their writing as a process of information dissemination. When they write, they first present the facts—what they have seen, heard, touched, counted, measured, or weighed—and they bring an impersonal analysis to bear on their concluding arguments. At their best, they can be succinct and to the point, ready with further information if needed. At their worst, they may neglect the subtle complexities of human communication, including ways to get their readers interested in what they have written. STs often exercise their preferences in fields such as business, management, accounting, production, the law, and engineering.

ISTJ

ISTJs prefer Introversion, Sensing, Thinking, and Judging. They are particularly adept at processing and analyzing large databases. Their writing often reflects a proclivity to understand the world through statistics. They want to be exact. In academic fields, they tend to be archivists, librarians, or empirical researchers who conduct experiments and then use the hard data to build their theories. In nonacademic fields, they gravitate toward technical professions, such as accounting, engineering, and the like.

ISTJs are reliable people who feel that one should work hard at the important things in life. Even though they usually do not like to write, they are often extremely productive writers. They dutifully work hard at writing (and at most other activities), and they are very efficient.

Part of their efficiency comes from what some types might regard as a formulaic approach to writing. ISTJs, when involved in just about any activity, want to find the right formula—the correct series of steps that will lead to a good finished product. When writing, they tend to search for a procedure that works and then stick to it. For this very reason, they often refer back to old papers or reports.

Writing Process

As with most Introverts, ISTJs tend to plan extensively, writing and revising in their heads, before they begin to put words on paper. This tendency to plan seems to be even more pronounced for ISTJs than for other writers. Their writing is often fully composed in their heads, sometimes even in complete sentences. Once they begin to put words on paper, they write very quickly, almost without thinking, and rarely revise. When they do revise, they tend to make minor editorial changes.

They will rarely write down outlines on paper, but they may outline in their heads. When working on longer, more extensive projects, they tend to put paragraphs on cards or slips of paper that they will arrange in a logical order and draw from as they write.

When they are writing for themselves, especially as mature writers, ISTJs follow their formula, or series of steps and procedures, generally without much variation. They are not ones to change what works. If they have always written with success on a typewriter, they are unlikely to change to a computer or some other new technology. When writing for someone else, they want to have explicit directions. Other types, especially Intuitives, might feel that ISTJs are not very independent or original. But they simply want to find the right formula. If they are not writing for themselves, they need to know as much as possible about the formula of the person for whom they are writing.

Atypical of most Judging types, ISTJs tend to start writing fairly close to the deadline. To others, they seem to be able to produce writing almost on the spot, but in fact they have already written completed drafts in their heads. When they begin to put words on paper, they write quickly, almost without stopping to think. They are very unlikely to stop to consider a unique approach to an introduction or an unusual word that will capture the reader's attention. Rather, they focus on clearly stating their information and ideas in a standard format.

ISTJs rarely revise for themselves. Once something is on paper, it is set. They might change a few words and correct some typos, but they will not usually rethink their entire approach. When writing for teachers or editors, they may need to revise, but they will find it difficult to do so unless they are given fairly specific instructions about what should be revised. They tend to believe that if expectations were clear at the beginning, they could avoid the messy business of revision later.

Strengths and Limitations

Although it may not feel this way to them, ISTJs are extremely efficient writers, perhaps the most efficient of all of the sixteen types. They are at their best when writing concretely—from facts, data, and authorities. Their writing also tends to be very clear, concise, and to-the-point.

ISTJs might become so immersed in their data that many readers, especially Intuitives, will have trouble isolating and understanding their central point. They may also overlook the human dimension of their writing and thus come across as too brusk, too dry, or sometimes even boring. They can deal successfully with this problem if they add a human element to their writing.

Natural Style of Writing

ISTJs often begin their writing with statistics, and the rest of their text may present more of the same. They generally prefer to write factual material over fiction.

Many types, especially NFs, feel that the writings of ISTJs read as mere outlines. ISTJs tend to rely heavily on enumeration, perhaps punctuating their ideas with "first," "second," "third," and so on. Their writing can often comes across as factual, objective, and analytical—too dry for many types, but to the point and clear for others.

Contexts for Writing

Student ISTJs tend to do best when they have teachers who give explicit, detailed, and clear directions. They find teachers who want every assignment to be unique and original exasperating. Mature ISTJs do best when they can follow their own agenda and do not have to adapt their content or style to variations in the taste or expectations of their audience.

They might find it difficult to write on topics or in fields that are highly abstract, such as philosophy or theoretical physics, or genres that focus on the expression of personal emotions.

Writing Blocks

Compared to other types, ISTJs seem to experience the fewest writer's blocks. When they do experience blocks, they tend to find a way to move on fairly quickly, even though it may not feel quick enough to them.

ISTJs will most often become blocked when they cannot find data or authorities to back up or to focus their initial ideas or beliefs. If they cannot find such supporting evidence, they might chuck it all and start over with a new topic. They also become blocked when dealing with a complex issue that cannot be easily broken down into segments.

Many of their blocks occur at the revising stage, when a teacher or an editor demands something different but does not clearly express where or how the text should be changed. If they are mature enough to demand explicit instructions, they can move on. When still immature, they more likely either ignore requests for revision or anguish over what changes they should make.

ISTJs can also suffer blocks when they are forced to approach writing in a new way, especially when this new way violates their personal formula for how to write. It is hard for them to write spontaneously, or to brainstorm, because they have not had a chance to think things through.

ISTP

ISTPs prefer Introversion, Sensing, Thinking, and Perceiving. As children, they are often those who constantly take things apart to see how they work. Their learning style is very hands-on, tactile, and active. When they become involved with a project, they will do so completely and with a lot of mental energy and intensity.

It is difficult, however, to tell where their interests will go. They are not the sort of people to have their life mapped out in advance. They may seem to spend most of their life relaxing, observing the world, and taking in data that might someday prove useful; yet they are drawn toward activities that produce a rush of adrenaline. They often remain an enigma, even to their closest friends.

As both Introverted and Thinking types, they are fierce individualists who are both selective and cautious about interacting with others. Because of their very casual and quiet approach to life, their natural strengths are often overlooked: a calm unflappability when things go wrong, an ability to hone in on a flaw in the system and to invent a quick solution, and the capacity to adjust to unexpected circumstances.

Writing Process

The writing process of ISTPs generally begins and ends in isolation. They are very unlikely to collaborate or even to seek out feedback on their drafts. Their process is also likely to begin with a practical problem that needs to be solved. Even when the subject of their writing is serious, they will generally see the entire situation as humorous and write about it with a great deal of irony and satire.

With everyday writing such as memoranda on the job and busi-ness letters, ISTPs tend to write off-the-cuff, quickly, and seemingly with little reflection. The apparent spontaneous nature of this writing may be misleading; ISTPs spend much of their life collecting data and thinking about what is important to them. When they have to write quickly, they can often do so with a surprising amount of evidence and facts to back up their arguments. For more extensive writing projects, they tend to plan extensively. If they do not have on hand the evidence and facts to support their arguments, they will thoroughly research the topic. Their research usually is a matter of getting the facts right rather than working on original theoretical insights. Getting the facts right might mean, for example, poring over spreadsheets so that they can state that *their* solution to the problem is the most effective or economically feasible one, and they will argue this down to the penny.

Unlike most Thinking types, ISTPs do not generally have a clearly mapped-out organizational plan when they begin to write, even though they usually think about their direction before they start. They tend to ramble, following the flow of their facts and data or the emerging plot of their satire. They expect to do many revisions, although they are usually based on their own rereading of each draft rather than on feedback from others.

While writing, ISTPs tend to focus on the content of what they want to say, thinking little about how their writing is getting across to readers or how readers are reacting to what they say. Readers are sometimes puzzled or annoyed by the writing of ISTPs.

As is typical of most Perceiving types, ISTPs tend to begin writing at the last minute. They seem to need to feel the pressure of a deadline before they can force themselves into action. They also keep many unfinished projects going at the same time, turning to one or another almost at random.

Strengths and Limitations

ISTPs tend to excel at humor, although their satirical pieces some-times come across as funny but without making a significant point. They also tend to excel at working with complex databases.

ISTPs may at times fail to soften or qualify their discourse, thus offending their audience. Their writing may appear to ramble and can seem rather unorganized.

Natural Style of Writing

ISTPs tend to write either biting satires or compendiums of facts and data and sometimes miss the connections or implications of the concrete information. Their satires often seem to exceed, or at least push the boundaries of, good taste.

Their organization may not always be very refined, so that their texts will seem to fall apart in places.

Contexts for Writing

ISTPs generally feel most comfortable when they are allowed to write what and when they want and are not pressured to seek feedback or make revisions based on this feedback. They can be rather defiant about not adapting to the expectations or demands of others, so they may find themselves at odds with coauthors, superiors, or teachers.

They will also find writing most difficult when they must write on abstract topics.

Writing Blocks

As is typical of most Introverts, ISTPs can plan too much and write mental texts that are never committed to paper.

Immature ISTPs can sometimes have trouble handling complex databases, although this is rarely a problem for more mature ISTPs. They may also become recalcitrant if an overly exuberant teacher attempts to draw them out of their shell by requiring writing that is too personally disclosing.

Whatever blocks they face, ISTPs best resolve them by giving themselves the time and space they need to do the writing at their own pace, on their own topic, and with no distractions from the outer world. A deadline set by others may help, but they need to approach the task and the deadline in their freely chosen way.

ESTP

ESTPs prefer Extraversion, Sensing, Thinking, and Perceiving. As writers, they are oriented toward experiencing the outer world through their senses. This makes them supreme realists, often living for the moment and, in the minds of others, often living on the edge. Because they see the tangible world clearly, their behavior does not appear as risky to them as it does to others. They are good-natured and like to solve problems spontaneously, especially practical ones. They can become impatient with long explanations—they would rather get down to the important details quickly and then get on with the job.

School settings for young ESTPs are often a real bore. They are more interested in the real thing than the theory behind it. They would rather see, hear, touch, taste, smell, or climb something than read or write about it.

They often learn the rules of the game only for the purpose of testing them. They love to troubleshoot a problem, make a brief recommendation, and then move on to the next problem. They are often friendly and enjoy physical activities, and they can be happy-go-lucky even in the most tense situations. Their friendliness leads others to like and listen to them, but they can be blunt at times. Because younger ESTPs become so caught up in the activity that draws their current attention, they may lack a long-range sense of direction.

Writing Process

ESTPs are not likely to be the type of writers who begin early. There is always something more interesting to do than write a paper that is due next week; besides, they rather enjoy the danger of putting a paper off until the last minute.

When filled with good intentions (or when feeling anxious about completing a large project), they might start to write early, but this premature draft rarely reaches completion. They will probably become diverted by a more interesting task, or they will organize themselves just enough to feel less anxious and then push the writing aside. They might be putting tremendous amounts of time into their research, feeling with each article they read that there is progressively more to read. However, they do not move toward closure or putting words on paper until the deadline is near and their anxiety is high.

When they do begin to write, it is almost invariably at the last moment. More experienced ESTPs have learned that, given their late start, they must make the first draft count. They thus invest a lot of energy into making the first draft good, making minor revisions and even editing as they proceed. When they put this much energy into their first and only draft, they are often reluctant to revise and may even express resentment toward teachers or editors who suggest revisions.

Once they begin, they prefer to work from facts and structure the piece by using a tried-and-true organizational format. They tend to write "linearly," making certain that each sentence is right before proceding to the next and revising and editing each paragraph before moving on. The slow-but-sure process can sometimes create blocks, for stopping to revise or edit might interrupt a flow of thought that can rarely be recaptured. The frequent stops in their writing and their tendency to develop ideas as they write often produces essays that move into unexpected directions. Even when ESTPs begin their writing with a clear sense of direction, it often goes elsewhere. As a result, early parts of an essay (say, the introduction) might not clearly relate to what follows.

Once they begin, ESTPs often find themselves turning out entire papers, maybe as lengthy as ten pages, in one sitting. They will, however, need to find little diversions, such as household chores, snacks, or a bit of exercise, to interrupt the solitary task of composing and to keep them at it for a block of several hours.

When writing longer pieces, say, a thesis or a book, their linear process usually does not work. When tackling such projects, ESTPs tend to spend a great deal of time taking notes on their readings, often in rather elaborate computer files. Recopying or keyboarding long quotes can help them understand the material, especially if it is highly abstract, and develop ideas. The quotes become the concrete data around which they form their writing.

When writing, for example, a hundred-page thesis, ESTPs can proceed more smoothly by thinking in terms of writing five twenty-page chapters. They might even work on several (or even all five) chapters at once, pulling in their quotes to get things started and, using a trial-and-error approach, shifting material from one chapter to another.

Strengths and Limitations

ESTPs are especially good at writing shorter pieces about facts in a set structure, say a news story using the journalistic inverted pyramid format. Their writing usually has a functional purpose—to communicate information, not to leave a lasting mark.

ESTPs often experience more difficulty with writing as the length of the piece expands. A short news article is easy; a dissertation is overwhelming. ESTPs can be overly critical or harsh in writing, and they might experience difficulty with abstract topics, although this becomes less problematic as they mature. More experienced ESTPs, who are willing to read and reread, will be more inclined to copy key passages and reflect on them and thus can easily handle the abstract theory that may have presented difficulty previously.

Natural Style of Writing

The nature of ESTP writing tends to be factual, analytical, and perhaps intensely critical or even dry. They use short, direct words and phrases—"nickel words" instead of "quarter words"—intended to give a direction or get a point across with power and emphasis. They avoid imagery or flowery language.

Longer pieces may lack coherence, with earlier parts not clearly connected to later parts. One sentence may not be clearly connected to the next and may slowly move off the established topic into a tangent.

Contexts for Writing

Although they may express dislike about deadlines, ESTPs usually perform better in situations where they write shorter pieces with frequent deadlines, such as in journalism and business, than when they are left on their own to work on longer pieces—say, in academic life, where they may have six years to build a publication record with little or no supervision. They like to reduce complex or technical topics into simple language that a layperson can understand.

When faced with unstructured writing contexts, they usually do better when collaborating with a Judging type, who can establish deadlines and help push the ESTP toward closure.

Writing Blocks

The greatest difficulty for an ESTP is getting started, and only a hard and fast deadline, externally imposed, will get them moving.

They might also lose their train of thought while in the process of writing, as they stop to revise or edit before moving on. Often composing rough drafts into a tape recorder can help with this problem.

ESTPs can also have difficulty sitting in front of a piece of paper or a computer screen for very long. There is always something more interesting or exciting to do than write. For that matter, there are always more interesting things to write, so they may abandon one project for another, starting many but finishing few. They are more likely to stay at a writing project until completion when they have a firm deadline and when they can select the right kind of little diversions or breaks. ESTPs need diversions that provide some variety but are not so enticing that they do not want to return to writing. Selecting the right diversion is a highly personal matter that each ESTP will need to work out for him or herself.

ESTJ

ESTJs prefer Extraversion, Sensing, Thinking, and Judging. They are highly responsible people who tend to work well within hierarchies. As managers or bosses, they easily move into the authority role. When working with their boss, ESTJs tend to show what they feel to be the proper respect and deference. Even within their families, they play their assigned role and expect others to play their role as well, although as children they might sometimes slip into issuing orders to their parents.

As writers, they also respect established roles. As students, they want to give the teacher what he or she expects. As writers on the job, they wish to meet their organization's expectations.

Although they do not always enjoy writing, especially when they feel that they have not yet developed adequate skills, they tend to perservere, working hard even when they are not receiving a great deal of positive feedback. They are also successful as public speakers, where they like to rely on experience and tried-and-true principles. Speaking in public helps them to get their ideas "out of their heads" in a forum where they sense its tangible force on an audience.

Writing Process

When ESTJs are assigned a writing task, whether at school or work, they almost immediately begin to schedule the assignment, often breaking it down into steps with interim deadlines for each step. They will even consider how this assignment needs to be balanced with other projects, limit commitments, rearrange social engagements, and do whatever is necessary to clear out the time to work on all the writing tasks and complete them by their due dates. They want to find out early on whether time and resources will allow them to work steadily toward completion by the due date. If not, they ask *then* for an extension.

ESTJs do not tend to wait for the muse to call or the deadline to near. They persevere with or without "inspiration." They can work close to a deadline when they have to, but they would much rather begin a project early so that they do not have to deal with extra pressure.

As they prepare to write, ESTJs do not tend to take a great deal of notes, nor are they likely to become overwhelmed in the research stage. They usually begin to write when they feel that they have a focus or a clear thesis that crystallizes the central point that they wish to make. For more mature ESTJs, this focus will include a clear sense of audience, which they tend to construct by thinking of a specific kind of person (a close friend or relative) who can embody the traits of the people they wish to address. This helps the ESTJ make decisions while writing a rough draft or, more importantly, while expanding that draft and refining word choice, sentence structure, organization, and so on. For example, when writing for a general audience of middle school students, they might think of writing the piece for their thirteen-year-old sister. As they write, they can ask themselves, Would my sister understand this word, or is it too sophisticated for her vocabulary?

When they begin writing, their research may not even be completed, but they will go ahead and push through a rough draft. The purpose of the rough draft, for them, is both to establish a structure and to get something tangible finished. By structure, ESTJs usually mean a clear point and supporting data that are arranged in some logical progression.

Developing a focus or central point for a piece of writing is difficult for ESTJs. They often do not find their focus until the end of their draft, but once they have it, their writing thereafter usually proceeds at a fairly quick pace and with few problems.

As they work through a first draft, often in a single sitting with few breaks, they work fast and try only to get key data or ideas on paper. They may leave unfinished sentences or gaps with notes that tell them what to fill in later ("put quote here" or "add facts").

Their rough drafts, often little more than prose outlines, generally require fairly extensive revisions. In the revising process, ESTJs tend to fill in the gaps, cut out excess words or material, work on transitions, polish sentences, and make sure their logic is tight. Much of their actual writing takes place after the first draft, but this is the process that tends to work for them. Once they have something on paper—the basic form of what they want to say—they are better able to make decisions about content and style. They often have someone else read their draft, particularly a colleague who is more familiar than they are with intuitive, academic, or abstract kinds of writing.

When they become tired of revising, feeling ready to move on, they will edit the piece and turn it in, often before the deadline. As a general rule, they are not overly critical about their writing. They are more likely to assume the attitude, I've done my best in the amount of time I had to write, met my deadline, and that's that.

Strengths and Limitations

ESTJs tend to be proficient writers who are good at reaching closure and meeting deadlines. As both Extraverted and Thinking types, they easily take charge.

They often excel at argumentative writing because they enjoy taking a strong stand on an issue and then presenting arguments and data to back up their position. They also excel at writing instructions or technical procedures with a practical focus.

ESTJs tend to do less well with personal narratives when the subject is the self or personal experiences. They also may not like to write fiction.

When still developing as writers, they may come on too strong, push their point too forcefully, or say things too harshly, and thus alienate their audience.

Natural Style of Writing

The texts of ESTJs tend to have a clear sense of voice—a conversational style that attempts to find ways of translating the spoken voice onto the printed page. As young writers, they often put words in capital letters, underline phrases, use italics or boldface letters, or use exclamation points to suggest their oral language. When more mature, their texts reflect spoken language in more subtle ways, say, in varying sentence structure, to achieve a clear sense of pacing.

ESTJs tend to write concisely, including a clear thesis and plenty of information and data. They do not like writing that is full of hot air or has little relation to real life. Theories are meaningless to them without real examples.

Contexts for Writing

ESTJs find it easier to write in contexts where they can express their opinions. They tend to find it difficult to write when their prose must strive toward neutrality. They like working with data and real-life experiences, but they also feel a need to include their own comments about or reactions to those data or situations. When working on creative writing assignments, ESTJs often feel as if they're required to write about something they've never seen, heard, or read before, and they usually need to find or develop a structure for how to get started.

Writing Blocks

ESTJs are most likely to become blocked when they cannot synthesize a variety of viewpoints or several abstract theories. They may also become stalled with what they call "ill-defined tasks." In such cases, they cannot find the focus that drives much of their writing process. They can most frequently emerge from this kind of block by talking about the writing assignment, especially with an Intuitive type.

Similarly, if they are unable to develop a clear structure as they write their rough draft, composing often halts. The more they can make ideas and data visible and tactile (say, by putting key points or facts onto notecards), the better they are able to work their material into a logical progression that they can feel good about.

They may also, especially when still developing as writers, become blocked when faced with too many stylistic or organizational options. Thinking about a specific person who represents their intended audience can usually provide a means of working through these kinds of decisions.

Four Sensing Feeling
Approaches to Writing

The four types of writers described in this chapter all share common preferences for Sensing (S) and Feeling (F). These individuals find out about the real world through directly observing it with the use of their five senses (S). They tend to make decisions based on what they care about, which invariably includes what others around them need and how those people feel about the outcome (F). As a result, Isabel Myers called these people the "sympathetic and friendly types."

SF writers see their writing as a means of connecting with other people and helping them feel better about their circumstances. They present the information they have about a situation that is most important to the people involved. In so doing, they may neglect to present a conceptual overview of their topic, that is, the big picture, or a logical analysis of the possible conclusions. But at their best, SF writers are good at determining what their reader wants to read about and at providing a story that explains what they have to say. They are naturally drawn toward caregiving activities, leading them into the health professions, teaching, religious and community service, and office work where people are involved.

ISFJ

ISFJs prefer Introversion, Sensing, Feeling, and Judging. Dependability is the hallmark of these types, who quietly accept responsibility and do as they are told, especially as young children. As adults, they often work tirelessly and unquestioningly in behalf of others. Once they promise a job will be done, you can go to the bank on their commitment. They also like to get their facts straight, and they lead their lives based on what has worked well before. Their practical

85

judgment therefore often leads them to be conservative and consistent. Around those friends whom they trust, they shed their quietness and can be surprisingly funny.

As students, ISFJ types are hard workers. They do not seek out leadership positions, but will accept them if asked. They tend to defer to authorities. They often seek work in fields that allow them to serve others in an orderly fashion, such as teaching, health care, or office work. They may take on too many tasks just because they were asked to do so and silently endure the burden without complaint.

ISFJs are not naturally drawn to writing. But when they do write, they see it as a means of self-expression, for example, writing in a personal journal that they show to no one.

Writing Process

As writers, ISFJ types start with the facts. They carefully collect information, often in file folders, on what has been written about a topic. When a folder is full, they lay out the many bits of information in sequence. Their first drafts are therefore often long presentations of data, which need to be condensed and summarized in a later rewrite. They have a tendency to restate what to others may be obvious, since they want to be sure they got it right.

ISFJs also like to establish, and follow religiously, a ritual for scheduling writing. At 4:30 every Tuesday and Thursday, for example, they may go to the same table or desk to find the tangible props—books, files, thesaurus, pens, paper, coffee mug—that assist them to write for a two-hour stretch without interruption.

If there are guidelines for an assigned writing project, ISFJs like those guidelines to be clear. If they are not, rather than ask for clarification, ISFJs often internalize their sense of confusion, thinking they are not good writers. When they do ask the teacher, boss, or coauthor to repeat his or her statement of expectations, they mean this literally. They want the restatement to be in the same words as before, which solidifies their sense that they got it right. If they are anxious about the project, a paraphrase will not do; it only increases their sense of uncertainty, since what sounds like new information has been thrown into the mix. They work best with quiet for concentration. When they collaborate, they do their best work alone before getting together with coauthors, which allows them to come to the session feeling more prepared.

ISFJs spend a lot of time thinking about what they are going to write. This prewriting phase is usually more effective when they attempt to think through the topic in a concrete, experiential way—perhaps visiting a museum to write about art or going camping to write about different species of birds. As is more typical of Extraverts, ISFJs also seem to benefit from talking about their topic.

Similar to their close cousin, the ISTJ, ISFJs tend to delay putting words on paper until close to the deadline. This does not mean that they are procrastinating. They are, instead, writing in their heads. In writing classes, they often resist writing rough drafts or working through multiple drafts. They prefer to be one-draft writers.

ISFJs write first drafts that include everything they know about the topic; then they refine their writing by finding conceptual themes and patterns in the material. In each draft they work solely on one aspect of revising—spelling in one rewrite, grammar in another, for example. Their perception of the draft itself is also building-block in nature; step one leads to steps two, three, and four prior to the conclusion. The five-paragraph essay suits them well: State the purpose of the essay, add three paragraphs of illustration, and then summarize the theme. Unfortunately, the opening purpose only becomes clear to them after they have the facts. They therefore should save writing that opening thesis statement until the majority of the paper has first been drafted out. If required to present the thesis first, they often report that they have to go back and change it after finishing the body of the paper.

When the first (also generally the last) draft is finished, ISFJs tend to have trouble rethinking it. Requests for broad revisions are hard for them to implement. They revise more extensively when they receive feedback that is very specific and directive.

Strengths and Limitations

ISFJ types usually write in ways that are clear, factual, and direct. They also often include human examples of the points being made. They rarely miss an important illustration or piece of evidence. Following formats that are already provided comes relatively easy to ISFJ writers, especially if the expectations are explicitly presented in advance.

Early drafts from ISFJ types tend to go on at length with facts and information without getting to the point. They usually have more passion and investment in their topic than shows on the page. They also have difficulty making smooth transitions from one section to another. Other types may tend to find that ISFJ writing restates the obvious. Imaginative brainstorming comes to them with difficulty, especially if done in a group; they work better alone. Critical analysis is also difficult for them unless they have a wealth of data on which to base their critique.

Natural Style of Writing

The prose style for ISFJ types at their best is simplicity. They prefer a narrative style that includes concrete observations and is based on practical experience. They do not engage in theoretical speculation but prefer to tell it like it is, often with warmth. They may understate the merits of their ideas and present the facts so that readers can come to their own conclusions.

Contexts for Writing

School or workplace writing assignments that have a practical function and a clear set of guidelines are favored by ISFJ types. They struggle if required to write speculatively or about things that are not real to them. They value explicit instructions and thus seek out teaching, health care, or office work settings where these values are more often respected. A writing environment that does not provide them with specific feedback on how they have done is problematic.

Writing Blocks

ISFJ types may be self-starters and will quietly persevere in working hard, but their work may be off task without direct feedback. Their blocks may not be apparent to others, since they persist in sticking to the job and do not easily seek out support or clarification, especially under stress. They also do not work well in a noisy environment, and interruptions exaggerate their anxiety.

To relieve blocks, or to avoid them in the first place, ISFJ types need to trust their need to understand clearly what is expected, ask for clarification when feeling uncertain, and start their first drafts with what they know for sure about the topic before moving into theory or compare/contrast patterns. They rely on past experience to tell them what works. They therefore work better when they know that either they or someone they know has succeeded at this kind of writing in the past and when they know exactly how this person succeeded.

ISFP

ISFPs prefer Introversion, Sensing, Feeling, and Perceiving. They are quiet but loyal followers. They therefore want to know what others require of them when they write. They are modest about their abilities and seek to please. In reality, they have greater potential as writers than they give themselves credit for. Their self-doubts come in part from the fact that writing is most emphasized in school settings, where there are relatively few teachers of this type, especially in colleges and graduate schools. ISFPs can be intensely self-conscious, and when presented with praise for a job well done, they often have trouble believing it.

As they mature, these types tend to gravitate toward human service fields where they are adept at noticing the tangible needs of others. They work, quietly and without fanfare, to meet those needs. Everything they do is from deeply held convictions, and they become personally invested in any project. They like to get their facts straight and often find theories puzzling unless they can be tied directly to the real world they have seen, heard, and felt.

Writing Process

Because ISFPs desire a solid relationship with those for whom they write, they can appear to teachers, classmates, colleagues, and others as lacking in ability as writers. This is not so. The misperception results from the important first step in their preferred writing process, which is to check, and doublecheck, with an authority about what is expected to be sure they got it right. Their tendency is to assume they have it wrong, especially in academic settings. They write with more confidence when provided with a model of a writing product that worked successfully in the past. However, they do not necessarily want to follow that model exactly, since flexibility is important to them. They usually check back with the authority about each adaptation they make.

The topic chosen absolutely must be one they care about, and preferably one about which they have some direct, hands-on, lived experience. They write best alone, but will want to touch base periodically with their teacher, boss, or coauthor to be sure they are on the right track. They especially rely on this feedback to help them in their revisions, which usually need greater organization. However, if feedback is too harsh, the ISFP may become blocked. Criticism must be accompanied by specific praise for the investment and seriousness that they have brought to their work.

Strengths and Limitations

As Feeling types, ISFPs write with warmth, dedication, and a gentle perceptiveness about what makes people feel motivated. They usually have rich experience in the tangible world from which to draw case illustrations for the material they write about. Their writing shows keen insight into the natural world of humans and animals, which they modestly tend to take for granted, assuming everyone has it.

ISFP types easily lose their sense of voice as writers and speakers, so attuned as they are to the needs and requirements of others, especially those in authority. Their early drafts may lack conclusiveness, since they tend to present too much data and too many options, leaving to the reader the task of deciding which ones are important. In revision, they often have to shorten their drafts, eliminating information that adds little to the overall purpose of the paper.

Natural Style of Writing

The writing style of ISFPs is usually explicit, leaving little to the imagination. They may tend to understate the importance of a point, even if they hold that value dear. Assuming they have freely chosen their topic, underneath the prose is a deep conviction in their writing. They tend not to discuss long-range implications until they have carefully presented the facts of the situation.

Contexts for Writing

ISFP types often experience academic writing with considerable agony and may need the one-on-one support of a mentor to survive. Dry theoretical analysis or argumentation can be a real struggle for them. They feel more at home in health and human service fields, business settings, or work with animals, where they can direct their quiet intensity toward helping others, and their writing usually needs to be geared toward the same end.

Writing Blocks

A pile of note cards, a stack of books or journals, and a formal outline on a computer may, by themselves, be a source of writer's block for an ISFP. What is missing is direct human contact or a reminder that a real world exists outside those abstract notes, texts, and outlines. A one-on-one conversation with a colleague, teacher, or editor feels more real and helps the ISFP regain enthusiasm for a topic. These conversations need to reconnect them to their need to view writing as a way to communicate to others the practical lessons they have learned about the topic they are writing about.

ESFP

ESFPs prefer Extraversion, Sensing, Feeling, and Perceiving. They tend to be easygoing, spontaneous people who are in touch with the here and now and interested in getting the most out of each moment. As children, they are constantly in motion and might be labeled as hyperactive. As students, they may view school as an excuse to party;

however, it is important to note that they apply themselves more to academics when they are involved in the social side of school. They also tend to perform better in real-life situations than on written tests.

Any social situation will bring out the natural gifts of an ESFP: friendliness, storytelling, jokes, and camaraderie. Their sense of fun, wherever they are, is neverending. The classroom and the workplace are no exceptions. They believe that even the most serious topic of discussion or reading can be made lighter with the right perspective. Unfortunately for them, few instructors in college are their type.

ESFPs do become more serious and academic as they mature. As this happens, they may feel that others do not take them—or their writing—seriously.

Writing Process

Getting started is usually the most difficult part of an ESFP's writing process, especially when teachers or bosses give vague instructions. They may have difficulty thinking of how their writing project will turn out, so they have little sense of how to begin.

They can generally come up with very good ideas as they talk about their topic with a friend, but they may not realize it. Ideas seem to come and go so quickly that the ESFP has trouble evaluating them or even remembering them. If the friend can listen and write down what seem to be good ideas, they can often find a starting point. If they cannot find a listener, ESFPs can often accomplish the same effect by talking into a tape recorder and then listening to their thoughts while taking notes.

Once ESFPs begin to write, they usually stay at it until the project is finished. They write in marathon sessions, which may last an entire day or night, partially because they only begin at the last moment but also because they have trouble seeing the writing project as having parts or sections. They begin writing, follow the flow of their thoughts, continue writing until they have said everything they can, and then they stop. They rarely have a sense of structure or organization as they write, which is often reflected in their rough drafts. Their essays, unless they have had time to revise extensively, can often seem to ramble without a clear focus.

The process of ESFPs usually proceeds more smoothly when they attempt to write quickly, without a great deal of stopping to select the right words or correct spelling and grammar. When they think too much about how their audience might react to each word or thought, they can become stalled. At its worst, their writing will slow to a few sentences or phrases scattered in spurts between long pauses. When they write in this way, their writing lacks cohesion or coherence.

ESFPs need to learn to start earlier so that they will have time to revise. They usually revise more thoroughly when they receive oral feedback that is very specific, almost directive.

Strengths and Limitations

ESFPs can often write moving personal narratives that are full of beautiful phrases—an almost poetic language. They usually do quite well at writing humorous pieces or relating anecdotes. As strong Sensing types, their drafts are usually filled with stories of real events or activities—a rich recounting of what actually happened, who it happened to, and how they felt about it.

ESFPs often struggle with traditional academic writing, such as research papers, critical analyses, and argumentative essays. Their writing may also ramble without focus, including a broad array of concrete stories or facts but lacking a unifying theme.

Natural Style of Writing

ESFPs tend to have a clear sense of voice and a vitality that is very appealing. Their style is conversational, and their writing often reflects their attempts to translate the spoken voice into a visual text; for example, they might use capital letters, underlining, or italics to suggest their spoken inflections and areas of emphasis.

Because they tend to write by following the flow of their ideas, they may connect one sentence with the next as one idea leads to another, but they can soon find themselves off the topic.

Contexts for Writing

ESFPs often do well in creative writing courses, as long as their instructors do not overly emphasis abstract ideas, and in other contexts that emphasize writing about values and morality.

They tend to struggle when writing about more analytical and philosophical subjects.

Writing Blocks

ESFPs experience more blocks when they do not write quickly. They often have trouble lingering over a single idea, so they tend to lose good ideas if they do not write them down quickly.

They can also struggle with trying to decide what kind of details should be included and which should be excluded. They write more easily if they save such decisions for a later stage of writing.

ESFJ

ESFJs prefer Extraversion, Sensing, Feeling, and Judging. They like to do things to help other people. Even as young children, they find great personal satisfaction in doing what is required to put others at ease. As both Extraverts and Feeling types, they are talkative, often popular, and are convinced that difficult times can be overcome if people only work together. They often become school leaders. They like to host social functions and, as hosts and hostesses, pay attention to even the smallest detail to make people feel welcome.

As students, ESFJ types therefore succeed through hard work and a supportive relationship with the teacher. At their best, they can put their learning to quick use in the service of others. At their worst, they may tend to doubt their own academic strengths, especially when abstraction and intellectual independence are required. They want to meet others' expectations so greatly that they often neglect their own needs.

Writing Process

As writers, ESFJ types work best when their first drafts are very personalized, showing what they care about. They tend to save until later the principle behind the anecdote. They thus need to revise their early drafts by removing excessive uses of the first person singular (for example, "I believe that...") and inserting near the beginning of their writing a general thesis statement about where the paper is going.

ESFJ types report that they love reading aloud and many also enjoy telling good stories. They also tend to like activities that bring people together to illustrate a point, such as coming up with the script for a skit. Many ESFJ types appear in the ministry and prepare their sermons with a noticeable warmth and personal touch to capture the attention of each member of the audience. Because they like to laugh, sing, and tell stories, at their best, their writing often captures this sort of around-the-campfire quality for their readers. They enjoy collaboration in all things, including writing. Indeed, unless they are working closely with other people—such as a teacher, editor, classmate, or colleague—they may feel stuck with their writing, finding the act of putting words on paper a bit tedious and dull. They would rather go talk with someone about their ideas or research than compose. However, if they are working on a required writing assignment, they prefer to finish the final draft alone, feeling distracted by the presence of others.

Strengths and Limitations

The writing of ESFJ types usually has a practical purpose behind it, often in service of other people. It carries a warmth of delivery and heartfelt conviction and is often punctuated with frequent stories or illustrations. ESFJs tend to cite other authorities in their writing, giving them credit where credit is due. They often like to write supportive personal letters of recommendation for people they know.

At times, the writing of ESFJ types may lack originality, authority, or the critical eye required of an analytical piece. Dispassionate categorization of data is their weak spot, since they want dearly to be personally involved in their writing. Unless they revise their first drafts, they may come across as trite, often with their feelings on their sleeve.

Natural Style of Writing

The natural style of writing for most ESFJ types is that of personal narrative: what happened, who was there, what I did in response, and how we all felt about it. Theory, abstraction, and data for their own sake are usually absent. Storytelling to illustrate a deeply felt moral is common in their writing. They like to communicate what they care about and value.

Contexts for Writing

The health professions, teaching, the ministry, and other people-service work all draw ESFJ types, and the kind of writing required in these settings usually suits them well. They write best when someone will take to heart what they have to say. They want what they do (including writing) to serve a direct and tangible human purpose, whether this involves logging in observations on a patient in an out-patient hospital setting or fleshing out the roles for a school play.

Writing Blocks

The biggest block for an ESFJ is indifference from others, especially pertaining to a heartfelt issue. If a teacher, colleague, or other reader of their prose neglects to comment on (or read) what they have presented, they are often visibly hurt and subsequently unmotivated to continue writing. They also get blocked by too many "shoulds," imposed either externally by teachers, bosses, or professional standards or by their own internal standards for themselves. In the interest of taking care of what others need, they may neglect to put into their busy schedules time to rest and take care of themselves, and their writing may reflect this lack of energy.

Blocks are best avoided or overcome by an ESFJ if they have a solid, direct relationship with their partners, readers, editors, or teachers. In the early stages of writing, they need to focus on what the audience expects and to write as personally as they know how, saving revisions for later drafts.

Four Intuitive Feeling
Approaches to Writing

The four types of writers described in this chapter all share common preferences for Intuition (N) and Feeling (F). Isabel Myers described them as the "enthusiastic and insightful types." They gather their perceptions by way of imagination (N) and decide what is most important about them via their personal value system (F). They see writing as a means of communicating the possibilities that humans have before them.

NF types bring a natural warmth to their activities and are deeply committed to what they do, including what they write and how they express it. They like to plumb the depths of previously unexplored territory, including human complexities, and usually have a gift for calling attention to subtleties in people's motivations that others might overlook. As writers, they may forget to provide a logical rationale or concrete examples to support their convictions. But at their best, they can be persuasive and inspiring in their written or spoken communication. As a result, they frequently find scope for their abilities in human service fields such as counseling, teaching, or the ministry, as well as in the arts, communications and journalism, and the behavioral sciences.

INFJ

INFJs prefer Introversion, Inuition, Feeling, and Judging. They tend to build theoretical models that relate to people and serve humanitarian goals. Like their close cousins the INTJs, they tend to develop ideas for a range of projects and feel frustrated that others do not share their vision fast enough. They are usually thinking about the next project before they have completed their current project. Unlike

INTJs, who tend to disassociate themselves from finished products, INFJs are more likely to feel personally connected to their writing long after it is finished and published. INFJs appear in significant numbers in education and counseling settings and in the clergy; not surprisingly, they are sensitive about both how others react to their writing and how their writing connects with and affects the lives of other people.

INFJs also tend to hold onto and nurture their ideas so intensely that it may sometimes be difficult to convince them to put these ideas into writing. Sometimes an extraverted coauthor, if he or she is a close and trusted friend, can help INFJs push more of their important ideas into their writing. The extraverted coauthor, however, has to respect the INFJ's need for space, even if this means that the INFJ's deep reservoir of ideas is never fully tapped.

Writing Process

As strong Intuitive types, INFJs begin writing with an abstract concept, which they want to bring to bear to help resolve or understand human issues. Their writing must also relate to their personal values. Any time spent on thinking and writing about why a particular project is important is usually time well spent: It may forestall a lack of motivation or writer's blocks later in the process.

As is typical of most introverts, INFJs like to spend a long time nurturing ideas before beginning to write. Although they might periodically talk to others about what they are thinking about writing, they generally prefer to develop their ideas in isolation and wait until the ideas are fairly well formed before they begin to put words on paper. Even though their first drafts are fairly polished and in a near finished state, INFJs are not likely to be one-draft writers. No matter how polished their first draft is, they want to spend more time getting the ideas just right, reworking words and phrases and rewriting sentences.

Once they begin to write a rough draft, they proceed planfully to complete the project. Shorter writing assignments might be drafted in one sitting; longer ones will usually be divided into sections and sub-sections so that a part of the text can be written each day. They design texts almost as an architect makes blueprints of a building, and their finished products are often, if only implicitly, divided into sections. Their writing has a narrative feel to it, including more attention to transitions and the overall flow of ideas.

Because INFJs hold onto their ideas, they are likely to produce fully developed rough drafts. Indeed, their rough drafts might be too long and need cutting. For the INFJ, this is a difficult task. Because they personally invest themselves in all aspects of their writing, it is difficult for them to decide what can be cut and what cannot.

When in the process of writing, INFJs attend to structure, but they are more likely to see structure as something relating to readers than as some abstract design. To them, the best structure is one that makes sense to the reader or makes reading easier or more enjoyable. INFJs derive much satisfaction in just knowing that their visions are shared with others.

In their drive to complete writing projects, INFJs are likely to view any interruptions from the outer world, including interactions with coauthors, as annoying obstructions. Because they value harmony in personal relations, they may be less quick than some other types to voice their need for space. This means that tension between INFJs and their coauthors can sometimes build until it is expressed in a manner that may seem out of proportion to the controversy.

Strengths and Limitations

INFJs are original thinkers who are skilled at personalizing abstract theories. Their writing, although on fairly abstract topics, is usually clear and can convey important implications for people's lives.

Because they live so intimately with their topics, INFJs can at times be reluctant to share even their best ideas. Also, their need to integrate all possible aspects of a topic into a piece can lead to drafts that may appear brilliant to some readers but incomprehensible to others.

Natural Style of Writing

The writing of INFJs tends to be naturally formal—the kind of writing that is typically found in academic disciplines—but with a subtle personal touch. Their writing is seldom dry or lifeless. People and personal values strongly come into play, if only implicitly.

Even though the writing of INFJs is, in general, clearly organized into topics and sections, these divisions are less logical than they are inspired by their broad vision of the topic. Despite the divisions, a basic narrative flow will often emerge.

Contexts for Writing

INFJs feel most comfortable in contexts that allow them to write about their personal values, that are open to new ways of looking at old problems, and that allow them the space to work alone.

They are unlikely to feel comfortable or do their best work when supervisors or instructors tell them how to write or when they receive harsh feedback on their early drafts.

Writing Blocks

One of the most frequently experienced blocks for INFJs is that they tend to hold onto their ideas too long before they begin to write about them. Often the encouragement of a coauthor can help them begin earlier.

As is typical of most intuitive types, INFJs can become blocked by trying to make everything that they write original and unique, even with common everyday writing such as drafting a simple memorandum.

INFJs might also become blocked as they attempt to find just the right word or phrase to capture the reader's attention.

Some INFJs report being blocked by deadlines, not so much those set by others as unrealistic ones set by themselves. They often try to say so much in a short space about a topic and its many implications that they become overwhelmed. Unless they pace themselves, for example, by setting a 5:00 P.M. stopping time, they can become consumed by their writing, even missing sleep.

INFP

INFPs prefer Introversion, Intuition, Feeling, and Perceiving. People often are surprised when they discover how deeply invested INFP types are in their work. They are usually quietly adaptable to the changing circumstances of life. But when important personal values are threatened, they stop adapting. As children or young students, they usually benefit from the teacher's support, but not in front of a group. As they mature, they want to have a subtle but meaningful impact on others and use writing as a medium to this end.

At their best, INFP types are warm, serious, and insightful. As strong Feeling types, they recognize nuances in the ways people look at things and express themselves, and they adjust their own responses accordingly. Their perfectionism is not about details, but about ideals. They are always on the lookout for a new way to inspire or improve their efforts, even when previous accomplishments have received wide approval. Harmony, peace, and deeper self-knowledge are their goals for themselves and others. They want to have a purpose beyond tangible rewards and often work in settings with little financial payback. They frequently take on more than seems possible to complete, but somehow get it done.

Writing Process

Agony is not uncommon when an INFP writes. The agony, however, when faced and accepted, can become pure joy. To them, words represent, however dimly, a deeper message they yearn to share. They may immerse themselves, heart and soul, into both their topic and the way it is being communicated. Their first drafts usually are, and need to be, lengthy. They seek to find just the right word to capture what they have to say.

Some INFPs radically revise each draft. It seems that they can never leave the project alone, even when it appears finished to others. When revising, they need to present factual data or illustrations of their original points, which tend to be abstract or rambling. They usually need to shorten their drafts, often deleting words, phrases, or sections that they have come to love. Therein lies another agony.

The INFP must, above all, feel personally engaged with the project. They have to care about what they do. They often love to write and seek professional work where they can express themselves by this means. Indeed, they often prefer to write notes, letters, or memos to colleagues or coauthors than to talk with them face-to-face. Extraverts especially may mistake this behavior as a lack in confidence; they should not. INFPs often have a profound commitment to every word they communicate.

Outlines work well for an INFP only if they are not formal. Instead, they dash off random thoughts about a project on pieces of scrap paper wherever they are, often while engaged in another project. After they retrieve these notes, reread them, and draw arrows among them, they can then begin to work on a semblance of structure. They keep several writing projects alive at once, at least in their minds, each stimulating original thoughts about the one they are working on at the moment. They refine projects into readable prose only as the deadline approaches. They love the challenge of finding connections across what at first appear to be completely unrelated sources of information.

Strengths and Limitations

INFP writing can provide just the right word or phrase to capture the attention of the reader. Their drafts also present meaningful connections across different sources. They usually write well on human interest themes, especially those on psychological or spiritual growth and insight.

The idealistic standards of INFP types may lead them to believe that their writing is not good enough as it reads now. Some will overrevise; others may abandon the project altogether. All will feel moments of intense inadequacy. Sentences, paragraphs, and whole drafts tend to be long and complex and must be condensed and simplified. INFP writers sometimes lose track of the central points of their content, since they focus so much attention on how it reads.

Natural Style of Writing

The writing of INFP types often shows a flair for word choice. It is also often original, artistic, or even poetic in style. Metaphors, symbols, and psychological images are common devices in their language. Though they use a lot of words to convey an idea, they avoid painting the picture too explicitly. They occasionally assume that the reader has more knowledge of the topic than he or she actually does.

Contexts for Writing

INFP writers thrive in an interdisciplinary setting. They like to build bridges across models. They therefore are often found in social science and humanities settings. Even in business or technical writing, they seek to address a wider audience and to inspire or motivate through their report. They can work at length without tangible support or financial resources and often fail to seek them out. They benefit from genuine warmth and support from colleagues, but the support is best communicated quietly and without public display.

Writing Blocks

Even a completed draft can be a source of writer's block for an INFP. It never feels finished or worded as best it could be. Reworking and revising come easily to the INFP, sometimes too easily for their own good. They have trouble with assignments that involve a mundane report of data or require a restrictive format. When a teacher or editor focuses on the mechanics of writing too soon, the INFP loses sight of the long-range theme. INFP types often imagine that their readers will be critical of their writing. They may also become blocked if they agree to too many projects that are all due at the same time.

Almost any block can be relieved by an INFP if they mentally describe or write about the block itself, including the feelings associated with it and the ideals lost in the shuffle. This gets their personal values engaged. Once a deadline realistically approaches, INFPs can tell themselves that the current draft is good enough—not ideal, just good enough for now. There is always time later for revising the draft, at least in their head. The ultimate audience, after all, is posterity, not the current reader.

ENFP

ENFPs prefer Extraversion, Intuition, Feeling, and Perceiving. They are inspired by possibilities, which for them usually originate in the outer world. Once they are inspired, they will work tirelessly—often past their physical limits. Inexperienced ENFPs may continue to push themselves relentlessly, even to the point that they are unaware of the internal sensations that signal impending illness. More mature ENFPs learn to withdraw periodically to refuel.

When involved in a project, ENFPs can be stimulated by difficulties, for each problem presents an intriguing puzzle to solve. When a project becomes routine, when their possibilities are reduced to mere facts, they usually become bored and seek fresh stimulation elsewhere. They may, thus, start many projects and finish few. As a student, an ENFP's greatest developmental task is learning to revise. As professional writers, their greatest task is learning to complete projects and push them through to publication.

Writing Process

Perhaps the most important element in an ENFP's writing process is inspiration. Without the intrigue of the possibilities of an idea or an unfolding text, writing rarely proceeds. They will most likely become inspired by ideas coming from the outer world—from experience or from talking to good friends. They often report that ideas seem to come from outside themselves, appearing magically on the page as if they had not yet thought them.

The inspiration on which they so depend can affect their writing process in different ways. Younger ENFPs, especially those writing shorter school assignments, often begin with a burst of energy, writing quite well for several pages until their writing begins to fizzle out. More mature ENFPs might write entire books in spurts of eight or ten pages that come out quickly during periods of inspiration. These pieces, which usually are not written in any sort of order or with any real sense of how the entire book will take shape, usually need to be rearranged and reworked into a coherent whole. Whether they get reworked or not depends on whether the ENFP remains sufficiently invested in the project or whether another intriguing possibility has captured their energy instead.

ENFPs often generate ideas by talking to others and may even compose collaboratively, talking out a text sentence by sentence with a coauthor. When writing in isolation, some ENFPs like to speak the first draft into a tape recorder. Others will draft on a computer or *freewrite*—that is, write by exploring ideas, throwing any and every thought down on paper. They prefer generating texts on a computer so their writing can keep pace with their rapid thought processes and because this method makes them feel as if they are interacting with another person on the screen. Freewriting is appealing to ENFPs because they prefer to leap into writing with little planning, generating text by trial and error. When they write with pencil or pen, their first drafts usually reflect this helter-skelter process—they are filled with cross-outs, arrows moving portions of text here and there, and insertions added along the margins.

The organization of an ENFP is likely to evolve organically during the writing process, even when they attempt to use an outline. They tend to discover most of their content in the process of writing as one idea triggers another. Indeed, some ENFPs have said that they only begin to understand what they have written after they or others read their text aloud, followed by discussion.

When they finish a draft, ENFPs often feel that they have not said enough. But rather than go back and compulsively revise the text, they are more likely, if students, to submit it unrevised or, if professionals, to leave it unfinished and begin a new project. They are better at finishing projects when they have a firm deadline, but even then they may wait until the eleventh hour to begin.

ENFPs are more likely to revise when they receive oral feedback or even when they read their text out loud to themselves. Much of an

ENFP's revision process is akin to translation. They may need to translate a chaotic first draft into a more polished finished product, a narrative or expressive piece into an expository structure, and a conversational style into formal prose.

Strengths and Limitations

ENFPs are creative and insightful, especially when analyzing people. They tend to excel at personal narratives. Their writing is usually original and complex, both in content and structure.

ENFPs may fail to complete writing projects or revise them. Once they have finished a draft, they might feel that a return to that text interrupts their momentum with other projects. They may attempt to accomplish too much in one project, making it difficult to begin or finish a task. Their finished products, if not adequately revised, may be poorly focused or organized and may include rambling complex sentences.

Natural Style of Writing

The writing of ENFPs tends to be narrative, expressive, and conversational. Usually, their style is more mature than that of their peers, displaying a striking and engaging use of unusual words.

Shorter pieces of writing may seem to flash in front of the reader with a burst of energy and then fizzle out toward the end.

The writing of ENFPs will tend to reveal a metaphorical, analogical (where one idea is associated with another even if not logically connected), idealistic thought process. They may even at times seem to symbolically fuse their sense of self with their subject matter.

Contexts for Writing

Nothing is more deadly to ENFPs than routine writing. They tend to find it difficult to adapt to contexts that value concise, factual, and rigidly formatted writing—the kind of writing typical in fields like engineering and business. They may also dislike abstract analysis.

They prefer to write only when inspired and on a variety of topics in a variety of styles.

Writing Blocks

ENFPs experience their major blocks when they are lacking in inspiration. When uninspired, they need to talk out their frustration with someone. They also need to try to find a unique approach to the task and find a way to relate it to their personal values—whatever it is that they hold dear in life.

When ENFPs are especially inspired, they may make their projects so large that they are simply impossible to complete. In such cases, they may need to seek help in narrowing their writing goals.

Undeveloped or young ENFPs may spin their wheels; that is, they may quickly generate a number of ideas but have difficulty focusing on any single idea. ENFPs may be able to reflect on ideas better by talking about them with a friend. They might also gain insights while relaxing in bed, taking a hot bath, or walking on the beach.

ENFPs may also become blocked when they have to write critically about others, even people they do not know or who will never read their critical comments. Likewise, they become blocked when they fear rejection from their readers, as when submiting an article for publication.

ENFJ

ENFJs prefer Extraversion, Intuition, Feeling, and Judging. They bring an infectious enthusiasm to whatever they do, and this includes writing. As both Extraverts and Feeling types, they are adept at being the catalyst for others to join the team or to be a part of any activity. Like their close cousins, the ESFJs, they may neglect their own needs in the interest of others. Unlike ESFJs, however, they will usually act on their need to be heard themselves. They like moving groups toward closure, but almost always after they've asked everyone in the group what they'd like from the outcome.

As young students in school, ENFJ types often become class leaders. They do well in academic work, not just through their individual ability but through their persistence. They like to arrange study groups and work well with company in the early stages of a project. Near the deadline, however, they need to work alone. As adults, they tend to enter human service fields. They are often effective as teachers, workshop leaders, or public speakers, and can motivate others through storytelling and inspirational ideals.

Writing Process

As writers, ENFJ types begin a new project through conversation. A first draft often results from discussion with others, and ENFJs like to keep in regular contact with coauthors, teachers, or colleagues with whom or for whom they are writing. They like to start early to get the writing project organized and under way and put a lot of energy in moving toward completion. They enjoy collaboration in all tasks, including a writing project. ENFJs naturally want to help members of the team work well together and find it very difficult when they don't. They try to arrange for everyone to handle the aspect of the task that suits them best.

ENFJ types often would rather talk out ideas than write them. But their need for closure may lead them to use writing as an organizational tool. They distinguish between the tasks of generating ideas, which they like to do with others, and the "serious" work of putting words on paper, which they prefer to do with no one around.

Their first thoughts about a topic, and often their initial drafts as well, need to be very personal, with their value system quite evident. Due in part to their need to have the paper finished, they may move rapidly from one idea to the next, skimming the surface of each. A single paragraph of their first draft might include a short phrase about a multitude of themes, loosely related. When they revise, they need to give each theme its own paragraph. But they also often need to prioritize among these alternatives. Organizing ideas in a sequence of importance or deciding which ones can be dropped altogether is a task that does not come easily to them.

Strengths and Limitations

At its best, the writing of ENFJ types is often motivational, entertaining, and anecdotal. ENFJs are hardworking and usually committed to doing the best job possible, even though they also like to have the job done. They usually have a gift for words, especially in speaking. Their writing often leads readers to feel as if they are attending a performance, with the ENFJ on stage making the presentation.

ENFJ writers may sacrifice depth for breadth in their beginning drafts and need to elaborate on distinct key points when they revise. At times, their writing is too wordy or conversational, and they may struggle with composition on technical or business topics. They tend to overpersonalize, using the first person singular. Writing a critique may be difficult for them, since they tend naturally to praise and support others' positions and can neglect points needing to be improved. Some get so caught up in an anecdote that they forget to elaborate on the theory it illustrates.

Natural Style of Writing

The prose of ENFJ writers tends to be uplifting, optimistic, and inspirational. They are quite expressive and operate comfortably in narrative writing. Their writing may be filled with personal illustrations of a broader theme. They like to punctuate key words or thoughts with exclamation points, underlining, or bold type. Hyperbole is a common device for them. They are naturally persuasive writers and like to write as advocates on human interest themes.

Contexts for Writing

A supportive relationship is essential between ENFJ writers and their audience, teachers, colleagues, or others who will read their drafts. This relationship should preferably be face-to-face. They write well in settings where their work serves a human function, such as in school or social service endeavors. Technical, business, or highly abstract academic writing is a struggle for them.

Writing Blocks

Indifference or emotional distance can drive an ENFJ crazy. Writer's blocks often result if the teacher, colleague, or boss is not available to discuss ideas throughout the writing project. ENFJs may also feel blocked if they made a decision about their topic too early, since they tend to stick to commitments once they are made, especially those involving other people. They usually prefer to talk about a topic or put it into practice with others rather than to write about it. In conversation, they can add on or instantly change ideas; writing seems to them so permanent.

Blocks such as these are usually overcome if the ENFJ can find personal sources of support along the way. Enlisting the help of a writer's group, a thesis support group in graduate school, or an individual they trust can relieve the block. At times, talking into a tape recorder can simulate the process of speaking to a group, and a draft can come from the transcript. Revising is much easier for them if they read the draft aloud to hear how it sounds.

Four Intuitive Thinking Approaches to Writing

The four types of writers described in this chapter all share common preferences for Intuition (N) and Thinking (T). Isabel Myers referred to them as the "logical and ingenious types." They gather perceptions through their imagination (N) and evaluate their ideas with logic and analysis (T). They approach writing as a means of articulating an original angle on their topic. NT types are generally willing to challenge authority or criticize points of view that they deem to have been weakly justified. In this regard, they value competence in themselves and others.

NTs often have an ironic sense of humor and a skeptical perspective, especially in response to ideas that are popular or faddish. As independent-minded as any of the types, they come up with new theories to explain complex ideas. In the process, they sometimes neglect to sensitize the reader to background information on or human examples of their concepts. At their best, however, they can present a brilliant analysis of the way a system works (or needs to work). They are often engaged in pioneering work, whether in technical, scientific, theoretical, or executive arenas, or in research, physical sciences, the law, or computer science.

INTJ

INTJs prefer Introversion, Intuition, Thinking, and Judging. As children, they often spend long hours drawing elaborate designs for houses or buildings. They seem to be more interested in these designs and the fantasies that evolve from them than they are in more practical and concrete activities such as building a playhouse or a model airplane. As adults, they continue to be fascinated with designs. In academic life, they are theory builders who often incorporate designs —flowcharts, diagrams, and schematic drawings—into their writing. In other fields, INTJs are often the persons who critique current procedures and design more effective ones to replace them.

As Intuitive types, INTJs are always searching for an original way to approach a task or solve a problem. They are theoreticians, but they do not like theory for its own sake. Supreme pragmatists, they want to develop plans, designs, and theories that work in the real world.

Writing Process

INTJs like to plan extensively in their heads before they put words on paper or enter them into a computer, and they tend to think about writing all the time, rehearsing bits of their current project in their heads. But they also like to complete writing projects quickly. Therein lies the central conflict for INTJ writers—they need time to think things through, but they also feel a need to reach closure. With many types of writing, they will frequently write only one draft, as when writing about abstract ideas or theories that they have thought about and researched extensively. When writing narratives, especially narratives that must be factually accurate, they are more likely to struggle through several drafts. They tend to design texts with a highly original, although very logical and orderly, structure.

INTJs tend to begin working on writing projects early, extensively thinking out their ideas and alternate wordings before they begin to write. They do, however, tend to begin putting words on paper early. As students, they may turn in research assignments weeks in advance of the deadline. As professionals, they tend to focus on one project at a time, while keeping several on the back burner.

While they prefer to think through a writing assignment before beginning to write, their drive to complete writing projects, which at times is almost obsessional, often leads them to start writing too early. They may begin to write before they have clarified their ideas or done enough research. When they are mature writers and know their subject matter, they will often write a rough draft before they have even done a review of the literature. When less mature, they may begin so early that they experience writer's blocks. When they experience such blocks, they need to learn to pull back and do more research or think about their ideas in more depth.

From the moment that INTJs make a commitment to a writing project (or from the moment that one is assigned), they begin to plan how it can be completed quickly and efficiently. Nothing ever happens fast enough for INTJs, but they are not the kind of writers to willingly enter marathon writing sessions. Once they have gotten control of their need to have things done immediately, they are likely to "chip away" at writing projects, reading a few articles or writing a few pages each day. Because they have planned the text thoroughly in their minds, usually breaking it down into a logical sequence of topics or sections, they are able to complete a project by writing it a section at a time.

Once INTJs develop their original structure, the logical sequence of topics or sections, their writing develops smoothly. If they begin writing before their structure is clear, they may experience several false starts, writing an introduction and then tearing it up, writing another, and so on. When they tear up these false starts, it is not necessarily because they are poorly written; rather, INTJs tear them up because they do not like the direction that the introduction is pushing them. INTJs, when writing, are constantly looking ahead, thinking about where each paragraph, if not each sentence and word, will lead them.

The rough drafts of INTJs, which are written quickly and expediently, are sometimes thin and need to be developed in subsequent drafts. For them, revision is largely a process of addition and expansion rather than cutting and polishing.

When working with editors or coauthors, INTJs will often feel frustrated by these "strangers" who intrude upon their writing process and slow it down. Lead, Follow, or Get Out of the Way is an apt motto for INTJs.

Strengths and Limitations

INTJs are original thinkers who have neat, orderly minds. They tend to excel at writing about abstract theories, especially when also critiquing widely accepted ideas.

INTJs can, at times, be too concerned about quickly completing projects, failing to thoroughly research the topic or to seek out reactions to their rough drafts. Some even report that they avoid others who may critique what they have written. They can be fiercely independent if under stress.

Natural Style of Writing

Of all the sixteen personality types, the writing of INTJs is most likely to be clearly and consistently organized. Sometimes their writing is too neat and orderly, too consistent and structured. They often produce dry academic treatises that fail to consider the needs of the audience. Many INTJs feel that it is enough to have good ideas and to present them clearly; they do not feel any need to "entertain" their audience. Thus, an important developmental issue for INTJs is learning to pay more attention to their audience.

Their writing is also likely to contain a number of bluntly stated comments or unqualified assertions. INTJs need to learn to recognize these and soften harsh statements or qualify bold assertions during revision.

Because they tend to write in segments, their writing often lacks skillful transitions.

Contexts for Writing

INTJs are fairly adaptable writers, but they probably find it most difficult to write when they do not have the independence to develop original ideas or an original approach to their topic. They can handle academic prose or technical reports as long as the writing process is largely within their control. When others are telling them what to write or how to write, they are likely to feel frustrated and experience writer's blocks.

Writing Blocks

The major block that INTJs experience results from beginning too early. When their writing is stalled, they need to learn to stop and wait.

INTJs also can become too locked into their plans. They may make decisions early on about how the writing project should be completed and then fail to reanalyze their plan as the project develops. It is important for INTJs to learn to be spontaneous—they need to stop at key points in their writing process, evaluate their progress, and then revise their plan.

As with most Intuitive types, INTJs can also become blocked while searching for a unique approach to the topic.

INTP

INTPs prefer Introversion, Intuition, Thinking, and Perceiving. They remain profoundly uninterested in an activity, including writing, unless it captures their unique sense of curiosity. However, once they begin to investigate an interesting idea, they become so captivated by it that they can lose touch with time and people. As young students, they rarely find in schools the kind of freedom to explore their interests alone, which is their preference. They can be quietly cynical, even as children, about showy displays of affection or by the praise of others. They usually have more important things to do than engage in casual chitchat or social gatherings. Unless the topic of conversation relates to something they have researched in some depth, they would rather observe quietly without joining the discussion.

Once in college or the workworld, adult INTPs gravitate toward fields where they can put their intense need to understand and analyze to the task. They work best alone but consult with others when the job requires it or in order to gain a deeper understanding of the principle behind their work.

Writing Process

As independent as any of the sixteen types, INTP writers compose best with quiet for concentration. They can become consumed by a writing project for hours (for adults, it may be days) on end. They thrive on the challenge of solving a new mystery or problem through their writing. A topic suits them well if it allows them to create mental models of how things work, sometimes accompanied by a new vocabulary to go with the model. As a result, they need to revise their rather lengthy early drafts, not only by shortening them but also by simplifying their sometimes very abstract or obtuse wording.

As Thinking types, INTPs prefer that required writing assignments have a rationale for the project. They need little or no stimulation from teachers to write and frankly are better off if allowed to go off alone to work on their own idiosyncratic idea. When engaged in collaborative writing, they absolutely need time to draft out their thoughts on paper before engaging their coauthor. They benefit from the dialogue, but they do their best thinking in isolation, after or before the interaction.

A prewriting strategy for some INTP types is to draw up a matrix of the essential points to be covered in each section of the paper. If four points are made in one section, four analogous points will be found in each other section. It is not structure for its own sake that matters, but as a rationale for where they are going. Indeed, they dislike formal outlines.

Whereas computer word processing has benefited many Extraverts because the monitor interacts with them as if it were another person, INTPs instead see the workings of the computer as similar to the inner labyrinth of their minds. Indeed, many INTPs have said that their idea of heaven is to sit before the screen with the door closed, the answering machine taking their calls, and the kids with a babysitter. The various documents, programs, or data sets at their disposal allow them to plumb the intricate depths of a new project. When composing, they may initially pause to reflect before typing a draft onto the screen, wanting instead to stare at a blank wall or to jot notes onto a legal pad. But once the writing process has begun, it is hard to pull themselves away from the keyboard as they work and rework their draft.

Strengths and Limitations

INTP writers can usually find the flaw in another's argument and will provide a corrective to it in writing. They often have a wry sense of humor. They are adept at presenting the conceptual underpinnings of a matter. They like to take extremely complex material and make it understandable without violating the complexity of the material or the system behind it.

INTP writers tend not to personalize their writing and, thus, may need to revise early drafts by introducing some human examples of the rather abstract principles they write about. At times their skeptical—even cynical—eye may produce a rather cryptic attitude toward the writing project, which may show in their prose as well.

Natural Style of Writing

INTP writing naturally tends to be expository rather than narrative. At its worst, it is overly academic and dry. At its best, it is incisive, original, and cuts to the essence of things. Some of the best investigative research is written in an INTP style. Logical criteria guide their organization. Their language may at times be technical, even when the topic or the audience requires warmth or subtle persuasion.

Contexts for Writing

The favorite setting for an INTP writer is one where there are few or no distractions and easy access to the resources they need. Computer hookups to library databases help a lot. They work best on projects where their capacity for analysis and problem solving are put to use, such as in academic settings or in any field involving theory.

Writing Blocks

Predetermined formats for writing are useless to an INTP. They will remain blocked unless they can originate their own. In serious or academic writing, they hate having to produce personal narratives or emotional expression, which they may deem to be superficial or irrelevant. Even with a topic they are engaged in, they may put off writing until they've read everything available on that theme. They can lose themselves in one project to the neglect of others that have to get done.

The best strategy for an INTP to overcome any writing block is to find a logical rationale to engage in the activity. Even personalized writing is possible, if a good reason exists to do so.

ENTP

ENTPs prefer Extraversion, Intuition, Thinking, and Perceiving. They like change. Almost anything new and unique will capture their attention. As a result, when they write, they like the variety and stimulation of topics that are new to them, and they look for an original angle on the topic. The quickness of their critical minds often leads them to enjoy debate, sometimes for its own sake, but mostly to clear their thinking. However, their zest for life may lead them to other interests, and following through on the details of an unfinished project is something they would rather leave for someone else to do. As a result, less pressing projects often do not get done until they become pressing.

As young students, ENTP types are often called impulsive, undisciplined and, at times, argumentative. As they mature, they find scope for their abilities in settings where they can consult or troubleshoot, quickly presenting their conceptualization of what needs to happen differently and leaving the follow-through to others. They think quickly on their feet and have an acute ability to see global patterns in a system. Discussions about abstract topics energize them. They tend to be visionaries, looking far into the future to imagine unthought-of ways the world might change.

Writing Process

Many ENTP types say they struggle with writing because they cannot sit themselves down to put words on paper. The problem is not that they lack ideas or words but that they do not like to sit. Standing, pacing, and, above all, talking are much more natural ways for them to generate ideas. The rather jaded view that many ENTPs have toward writing usually results from traditional composition instruction in elementary schools, which demands detailed outlines, quiet for concentration, and a methodical process. None of these suit the ENTP. Dictating or tape recording their extemporaneous discussions or presentations (they enjoy presenting to groups) can help them begin the process, as long as someone else will put it on paper. A transcript of these talks often serves well as a rough first draft.

Because they are so often engaged in multiple activities, ENTP types tend not to turn to the words-on-paper aspect of writing until a deadline looms. At that point, they often need to go off alone, lest they become distracted by the presence of others. Revision usually requires that they attend to the mechanics of writing, which they neglect until then: protocols for organization, spelling, grammar, or punctuation. If required to present an outline, they prefer first to write a rough draft. Many ENTPs comment that outlining what they have already written helps them bring structure to their early thoughts. For younger ENTP writers, facts and personal illustrations do not come to their minds first and must be added to a later draft. In collaborating, they tend to want to leave to colleagues the tedious tasks of checking for correct citations or proofreading.

Like INTPs, many ENTPs have found the invention of computer word processing to be a long-overdue boon to their writing. Unlike their Introverted cousins, however, the computer, to an ENTP, is less of an intricate analyzer and organizer than it is a means for bouncing from one interesting possible theme to another. The process for them somewhat simulates a group brainstorming session, with the interactive audience somehow transformed onto the screen, giving immediate reactions. Also unlike most Introverts, the ENTP will not mind composing early drafts while also talking with a colleague, either on the phone or standing behind them as they type. The more external stimulation the better, at least to get the process going.

Some ENTP writers have been known to compose while standing up, with a tabletop adjusted in height to allow them to move about easily as they write, pacing if necessary. They like to remain physically close both to their writing and to the world around them, which has provided the necessary stimulation to write.

Strengths and Limitations

The writing of ENTP types demonstrates enthusiasm for new conceptual models, the more complex the better. Intellectually, they are system builders and problem solvers. They have a capacity to find the flaw in an argument and to point it out forthrightly. Critical analysis in their writing tends to come easily as a result.

They tend to write and talk with a playful sense of humor, teasing others who get stuck in mundane routines.

ENTP types can at times overstate principles without supporting evidence. Their language may be insensitive to the reader's need to understand the background information. They can present compelling reasons to support their vision but may appear to others as not interested in contrasting data, only those that prove their theory. In fact, they relish a competently presented contrasting view, even though they may initially argue against it.

Natural Style of Writing

The style of prose for an ENTP is often intellectual, inspiring, and challenging of orthodox views of life. They are adept at critical analysis and argumentation. They also thrive on coming up with new conceptual models. Their language can be witty and playful, sometimes at others' expense, sometimes at their own.

Contexts for Writing

Formal school settings are troublesome for many ENTP types, especially younger ones. They need room to run, play, tease, argue, challenge, and create new ways to do things. They learn and write best in environments where teachers and peers give them room to roam, challenge them back without fencing them in, and ask for more (and more!) of their thoughts about any topic. No challenge is too great for them when inspired. They thus gravitate toward work settings involving organizational development, consultation, scientific research, marketing, or promotion. They like to use computer word processing once they see it as a live, humming, responding creature with whom they can have a dialogue.

Writing Blocks

An ENTP will lose interest in a writing project if it does not stimulate their imagination or if it requires too much routine in the early stages. A quiet corner of the library may be the worst possible environment for an ENTP to find inspiration; they prefer an on-line search where the computer responds quickly to their inquiry and will print out the list of sources. A lively discussion with someone else taking dictation also suits them well. If their autonomy is not acknowledged, they will avoid a writing project if possible or redefine it to their liking. Pleasing the teacher, boss, or colleague for its own sake leaves them absolutely cold, and sometimes provokes from them a playful subversion. Required outlines in advance of a first draft have a similar effect. Sometimes, their minds run to too many options because they feel constrained by the task of narrowing to one.

These blocks can be overcome as long as the free spirit and sense of autonomy of the ENTP are engaged. Challenging their thinking may lead to an immediate retort, but in the end they feel respected and are often stimulated by the challenge. For young ENTP writers who face too many topic options, diving almost randomly into two or three of them, especially in conversation, can often lead to what may appear to be a rather arbitrary choice of one. But the process has begun, a focus is accomplished, and the block, at least for now, is set aside.

ENTJ

ENTJs prefer Extraversion, Intuition, Thinking, and Judging. Both as children and as adults, they are natural leaders. Their writing, therefore, is often designed to show their readers ways to be more productive. Logic dictates to them that the best approach to any task is through organization. They value competence, and they get things done. They are competitive and accomplish their goals through taking charge of the world around them. They like challenges, including intellectual ones. The language of ENTJ types usually demonstrates their broad possession of knowledge and their confidence that they have it right. Both in speaking and writing, they may appear more confident than their actual experience can support.

Writing Process

ENTJ types usually write their first drafts from a brief outline. They start with a sense of direction: If A, then logically we can expect B to follow. A pad of blank self-stick removable notes, a pen, and several sheets of paper often serve as the props for their organization. Only a single idea goes on each note. Once a page is full, the ideas can be easily rearranged to set up the first draft of the paper.

Revising usually requires that the ENTJ expand on an idea presented too superficially in the first draft. They have a tendency to focus on their message and its importance more than on how it needs to be expressed to reach the audience. Therefore, they must often qualify or soften overly blunt statements and find ways to build a warmer connection with their readers. This is especially important if their readers include opposite types, whose sense of authority and confidence are usually less firm than theirs.

If they collaborate as writers, ENTJ types naturally take the lead in structuring how the team will work. They are willing to write the first draft or to decide what tasks will be delegated to whom. They also take charge of time management so that any project can move steadily toward completion on schedule. A pitfall in collaboration is that they may put excessive pressure on others—as they do on themselves—to perform to the highest possible standard.

Strengths and Limitations

ENTJ writers are well organized and usually get to the point quickly. They can easily point to the essence of what was missed in another's argument in a few concise words. They like the challenge of wading through complex issues in order to identify the crux of the matter.

The writing of young ENTJs may often be terse, blunt, or too brief. It may need elaboration, especially with human examples. ENTJs may also rush to judgment about the topic of their writing and can become impatient if their instructor, editor, or other initial readers do not give them immediate feedback.

Natural Style of Writing

ENTJ writers use language that is frank and to the point. They are adept at writing directives that include itemized notes on how to put a method into practice. They do not beat around the bush. They write analytically and dispassionately and usually have factual evidence to support their arguments. There is a natural sense of cadence and punctuation to their prose, since they focus on how the message sounds as much as on how it reads.

Contexts for Writing

Most ENTJ writers need to be in command of their own fate, even as children or young students. Leadership roles and administrative positions thus allow them to write in the service of directing events and getting things done. Even when not in leadership roles, they value having an organization operate well and, thus, like to write manuals or technical reports, as long as they can produce a long-range vision along the way. In academic settings, they enjoy restructuring a web of complex theories in order to bring clarity.

Writing Blocks

An ENTJ may lose interest in writing if it does not serve a purpose, especially one leading toward clarity or efficiency for the reader. Personalized journals or poetic expression of heartfelt emotions, if required, will leave them cold. They may also become blocked if their coauthors, teachers, or editors are not as punctual as they are about getting organized and responding to initial plans or drafts. Another common block comes from foreclosing too soon on the topic and the thrust of a writing project before gathering enough information about possible directions. At times, ENTJs are harsh in their self-criticism, valuing the highest possible standard of performance.

These blocks are best overcome by ENTJs if they can include in their plans some room for the unexpected and for the possibility that a change in focus might, later on, be wise. Whenever they can be fully in charge of the project, their need for mastery and achievement will be honored. While they may hesitate to seek others' feedback if blocked by their own inner critic, they usually benefit from a realistic appraisal from someone they respect.

PART IV

Practical Applications

❖❖ Knowing about and understanding your personality type can be a real gift to you as a writer. You can relax, having discovered that your secret "tricks" are not odd or abnormal but are natural extensions of who you are as a person.

Knowledge of your preferred writing process can be practical as well. In this next section, we will provide examples of how you can draw on these natural preferences to solve problems at various points in your writing, such as finding and expressing your "voice" as a writer or your natural style, drafting and revising a particular writing project, going beyond your preferences to grow as a writer, overcoming writing anxiety and writer's blocks, adapting to the requirements of different audiences and writing settings, and writing with coauthors or collaborators of varying personality types.

Your Natural Style
and Its Consequences

The idea that individuals have a kind of natural style of communicating, a way that seems related to their personality type, is not new. Over two thousand years ago, Aristotle described how the speaker's personality enters the speech and how that "character" in the text affects the listener's willingness to believe or doubt the speaker. Today, writing specialists often encourage people to find their "voice" as they write. This metaphor suggests that the author, when he or she is writing well, breathes life into the text.

In this chapter, we will refer to this distinctive *character* or *voice* that enters your text as your natural style. Jung's type theory can help you recognize how your personality is connected to the strengths of your style.

In order to explore your natural style or voice, we would like you now to write a page or two about a specific set of observations you will make. Take a notebook with you to a local park or other outdoor place, find a comfortable place to sit for ten or fifteen minutes, and take notes on what you observe. Then write a narrative describing what you noticed.

You will be able to compare your essay to the essays of four students as we demonstrate their natural styles. We will also present the reactions of other students and teachers to these essays. The readers were asked to respond not only to the essays but to the writers and their imagined characteristics.

The following four essays were written by students who were studying the writing of history in a college freshman composition class. Like we have asked you to do, they too went to a local park, observed what was going on, and took notes. Their instructor then asked them to write a narrative, a kind of history, about what they observed. As we will see, these students took the same reality, the same "historical record," and wrote very different accounts of it. Their personality played a major role in what they saw in the park, how they interpreted it, and how they wrote about it.

The Natural Style of STs: Linda's Essay

Linda wrote an essay that reflects the typical values of Sensing Thinking (ST) types. It focuses on the things in the park, which she describes with scientific accuracy. Her frequent use of "I," usually in a phrase like "I see" or "I observe," does not make the essay more personal, as one might ordinarily expect. Rather, it seems to reinforce the essay's objectivity, increasing the distance between the observer and the objects that fall under her analytical gaze. As she catalogs detail after detail, she organizes in a spatial pattern, which is perhaps most clear in the second paragraph of the essay:

> Today, at 10:30 A.M. on October 20, 1988, I decided to spend about forty-five minutes at the Robert W. Woodruff Park. The temperature is about sixty-two degrees Fahrenheit, with partly sunny skies and very strong breezy winds.
>
> As I sit down on a bench, I notice immediately how the small park is shaped almost in a figure eight. Around this figure eight there are two different types of lamps. Inside the figure eight there are lamps with circular objects on top, and outside the figure eight there are regular streetlamps; on one of these, a pigeon sits. Speaking of pigeons, two students who are eating food from the local fast food restaurant, McDonalds, are surrounded by hungry pigeons begging for food. I cannot help but laugh along with the other people around me.
>
> Next, I admire some more of the scenery within the park. I notice that flowers are still blooming and the trees also seem to have all their leaves, even though it is late in the season. The bushes also seem to be cut evenly to produce some shade, while the sprinkler system seems to be watering them.

As I admire what is going on outside the park, I notice all the buildings surrounding me to my right. I see the sign above the Fulton Federal Bank, which shows me it is now 10:54 A.M. Next to that is the 7 to 7 News stand, Hardees, Blimpie, GNC, The Foot Locker, Kentucky Fried Chicken, and Hardy Shoes. To my left, I see a Pearl Vision Center, Muses, and the C & S Bank and clock. Straight in front of me, I notice a Chick-Fil-A building with a Canadian flag flying above it, a building that looks like a piece of cardboard, which is the Georgia Pacific building, the black Equitable building, and the Company of Georgia building with the United States and Georgia flags flying on it.

The streets that surround me are Edgewood, Park Place, and Peachtree. Some of the street signs include One Way, Do Not Enter, and Walk and Don't Walk, which is right in front of McDonalds. Parked in the street is an ambulance, a police car, and a Wells Fargo truck. I can hear sirens and horns off in the distance.

Then I turn my attention back to the people in the park and notice a man on crutches making his way slowly from one end to the other, a few businessmen, probably going to lunch, and a couple of students who appear to be shivering. I also notice a man walking his little child around the park, a policeman sitting on his motorcycle, and a student making conversation with the policeman.

Over to my left, I notice some rough-looking people gathering on a bench. They appear to be friendly; they are speaking to a child of about six years of age, who is not responding. A woman walks up to the men on the bench, and I cannot help but notice her hair—it looks like a wig. I know for sure it is a wig when her friend adjusts it for her. The people on the bench begin to drink some sort of beverage wrapped up in a paper bag, which I assume is alcohol.

Finally, it is now 11:14 A.M., and I decide it is about time to head on down to Five Points to watch the construction of Underground Atlanta; then I'll be on my way home.

We can certainly point to the precise observations and objective listing of details as strengths of this essay. However, it is not exactly a narrative, a form of writing that STs often find difficult. Nor is it very personal, which is also often difficult for naturally objective and analytical STs. Linda is the type of writer who finds it easier to be precise, objective, and analytical. She is more likely to feel comfortable with the kind of technical reports typically required of scientists, engineers, or accountants, all of which are careers that attract STs in large numbers. She is more likely to struggle with creative writing (the major exception, for some STs, being satire), personal narratives, and writing that deals with abstractions or ambiguities.

When readers reacted to Linda's essay, they felt that she was the kind of person who was under tight controls, who did not express her true self. One person described her as being a "female Clark Kent." A number of readers described her as wearing "neatly pressed jeans." In some writing contexts, the objective and factual style of STs is highly desirable. In other writing contexts, those that demand a more personal response, STs need to learn to be more expressive; this can often be accomplished by using more personal examples.

The Natural Style of NTs: Jeremy's Essay

As an Intuitive Thinking (NT) type, Jeremy tends to write both abstractly and objectively. As you read the following essay, note how much of his essay focuses on the *concept* of history:

> *History, or what we define as history, is not merely a past occurrence, or a set of events that happened in a previous time. History, rather, is a constant, a continual happening that affects each individual separately and differently. History as a tangible concept, therefore, is how a certain moment in time affects an individual, group, or specific object. History encompasses everyone and everything, whether sentient comprehension is possible or not. History is "physical" study, residing in all, affecting all, resulting in some sort of outcome, whether it be grand in scale or minute by comparison.*
>
> *Our assignment is to view the events we encounter from spending an hour in the park. Remember, if an event happens, whether or not it is retained as a factual happening is irrelevant to the fact*

that the event is still history. Whether it lasted a second, a minute, or longer, something that happened in that day's present will be history when that happening is over. Entropy, for instance, is a direct counterplay to history. For example, an event happens, is completed, and is remembered; then entropy or change is what follows, thereby giving the individual the ability of hindsight— reflections on the past events.

A Day in the Park

11:00 A.M.: The first thing I do is look around, get acquainted with my surroundings—get a feel for the rythmn of things—then I look. I see an assortment of street dwellers—history they will remember of themselves, but hardly recountable on a more all-encompassing view. I see pigeons, the grass—still wet from the sprinklers being on. I look up—buildings—definitely history that can be related to by a more general audience, from the people who built them to the people who owned or own them to the employees working in them. I see the flag, another definitive historical landmark that a general audience can appreciate, whether they be foreign, naturalized, or native. An ambulance races by. Everyone stops to look—the human penchant towards crises. It is history to us in the sense that we remember that there was an ambulance that passed on this day, but even more historically significant to those in the ambulance. I see busi-nessmen and women, I see students—all this will be history to them, to us. History is a relation between man, woman, and any other sentience able to comprehend the past, in his/her/its memory. History is memory, but memory is not history; the two are often confused, leading way to human interpretation where instead factual documentation is needed.

Jeremy is certainly less attentive to the concrete details of the park than was Linda. When he includes them in the second part of the essay, they are secondary to the abstract idea of history that he wishes to explore. He also employs an unusual vocabulary, such as "sentient" and "tangible."

It will perhaps come as no surprise that NTs like Jeremy tend to be theoretical model builders. They are, in other words, the people who like to explain how something works, and their writing is often accompanied by diagrams or flowcharts that illustrate some complex process, even as grand as how the universe was created. People of Jeremy's type tend, not surprisingly, to go into fields like theoretical physics or philosophy. In any field that they enter, they tend to gravitate to its most theoretical side. If they become psychologists, for example, they will be more interested in building a model of the psyche than in running experiments with laboratory rats.

When students and teachers react to Jeremy's essay, they see him as being highly intelligent, some imagining that he wears "John Lennon–type glasses." But students and teachers were often annoyed with Jeremy's writing, feeling that he was obnoxious with his knowledge, a bit of a showoff. Some even described him as a nerd, a common response that is issued as a defense against those who flaunt their intelligence.

If Jeremy is going to learn how to write less offensively, he will need to learn to use his intelligence without coming off as a know-it-all. He will, in short, need to learn to be less authoritative. He would do well to present an image of himself that reveals some uncertainty, perhaps by using phrases like "I believe" or "I think." He will also need to learn to meet the reader halfway by explaining some of his more esoteric theories and toning down his vocabulary. Then his readers will be more likely to view him as a sage—despite his youth—rather than as an annoying nerd.

The Natural Style of SFs: Robin's Essay

Both Linda's and Jeremy's essays were relatively objective, focusing on either objects or abstract ideas. Robin's essay, however, is subjective, focusing instead on the people in the park. Robin is a Sensing Feeling (SF) type.

> *It all started at 10:25 one morning in Robert Woodruff Park. It was rather cool that morning. Your typical fall day. It was like a picture on a Thanksgiving greeting card. The park was rather empty this time of morning. There were a few people seated at different*

places in the park, as if they were in their own little worlds. The pigeons were up and about; they walked anxiously about, as if they were expected to do whatever pigeons do. This was to be a morning I would never forget.

As I was observing what was going on in the park, a man walked up and started talking to me and the others who were with me. At first I thought he was somebody who just had nothing better to do than bug us that morning. To my surprise, he was the park maintenance man. His name was George. George was very interesting. He knew everything about the park. He knew about the sprinkler system, because he turned it on while we were seated near it. George could tell you all about the people who visited the park and the ones who made it their home. After all, he had been working there for over twenty years. He told us all about the park, the people who were there that morning, and his life and even tried to give us advice on how to live our lives. George was just one of the people I saw that morning. There were many others.

As time went on and it was nearing the lunch hour, more people were passing through and stopping in the park. There were lots of businessmen who, I noticed, wore the same style of shoes. It must be the "in" thing to wear for businessmen. There were homeless people seated or sleeping on benches as if the benches were their personal domains that they dared anyone to try to enter. Some people were in the park talking to others, to themselves, reading, eating, or just enjoying being outside. A man I saw seated under a tree was so happy he was talking to himself. One person I noticed who was not too happy was a man pushing a grocery cart. He pushed the cart into another man and greeted him with profanity—now that was not a gesture of happiness.

As my morning in the park came to an end, there was one more thing that I had noticed earlier about the people passing through the park, especially the women, that was more apparent now, since more people were passing through. They all seemed to look down at the ground, as if they were scared to look up, frightened of what they might see. Things really aren't that bad there. You might find things a bit interesting—like I did.

When my time had ended in the park, I told my new friends—
George and the other people—and the park farewell and went on
my way.

Of the four essays presented in this chapter, Robin's is most clearly a narrative. Her essay reads like a miniature myth. She begins by describing the park like "a picture on a Thanksgiving greeting card." She ends by writing, "I told my new friends—George and the other people—and the park farewell and went on my way." Although she is clearly writing about real people in a real place, her essay also seems to become larger than life. The mythic feel to this essay stems from her natural optimism. She saw the park, in the view of many of her classmates, as being better than it actually was. Even though during the hour that the class viewed the park, a man urinated in full view of the class, and even though the park was dirty and a bit dangerous, Robin saw it as the kind of scene that might appear on a greeting card.

This kind of optimism that often accompanies the writing of SFs can lead others who read their prose to view them as being childlike. And, indeed, SFs often feel that they are not taken seriously, that they are often viewed by others as naive. In some kinds of writing, the SF's ability to tell stories is a real strength. Many writers of popular fiction are probably SFs. They also excel at the kind of writing done in the helping professions, such as health care, teaching, and social work, explaining, for example, how to handle a particularly difficult on-the-job case. But with other kinds of writing, especially academic writing, SFs will need to learn to be more critical and less optimistic.

The Natural Style of NFs: Susan's Essay

Like Robin, Susan wrote an essay that was more personal and more people-centered, but with a difference. Susan, an Intuitive Feeling (NF) type, was less concerned about constructing a story about the people in the park. She was more interested in exploring her impressions of the people she encountered.

That day in the park two main ideas kept recurring in my mind: how our lives are so self-centered and our right to individualism. Most of the people I observed were either too absorbed in themselves to pay attention to their surroundings or they just didn't care what people thought of them.

For example, there was one older man sitting on a park bench dressed in his Sunday suit and hat. I doubt that he even noticed us observing him. He was just sitting there enjoying the day and feeding the pigeons. It's amazing how many of us become so involved in our own lives that we are blind to the simple things in life.

Businessmen walked by several times—they seem to be the best at ignoring their surroundings. They walked by seemingly unaware of the football game with the pigeons that was going on, the man playing a guitar, the window cleaner scaling the building, or the man preaching about the end of the world. Maybe if we took the time to look around at other people or our surroundings our lives wouldn't seem so complicated or troubled.

Individualism involves the right to be ourselves, but not to become so self-involved that we begin to ignore others. Many of the people I saw were exercising their right to be themselves. The man preaching was the most obvious; he wanted to preach and felt what he had to say was important. He wanted to share his thoughts and beliefs with the public. I find it odd that in a country that professes freedom of speech, a man is stopped by an officer of the law for speaking openly.

Another man was simply spending his day with himself, absorbed in his own thoughts. He carried on many a conversation and song with himself. I really don't think he cared what anyone thought of him or what he was saying. He was happy doing what he wanted to do, regardless of what anyone else thought.

I guess that everyone's perceptions are different, but I don't understand how people can ignore life around them. Those people in the park—like the man preaching and the older man—I envy, in a way, because they're doing what they want regardless. They don't seem to be so impaired by society's regulations.

Susan is, like Jeremy, interested in ideas (an influence of their shared preference for N), but there is an important difference between their two texts. The park is important to Susan because it evokes certain reactions in her. She is not exploring an objective idea, like the meaning of history; rather, she is exploring how events affect her. Her essay is both abstract and personal.

Susan's text, which might seem freeflowing or even disorganized to many, has its own kind of structure. She is clearly exploring ideas and following the flow of her thoughts; the structure that emerges from this process is one that has more to do with the association of like ideas (a trail of thoughts, if you will) rather than the arrangement of ideas into clear categories. When NF writers are thinking clearly and their ideas are leading into one another and leading toward some conclusion, their papers will flow well and will be coherent without being overtly organized.

Perhaps because of this freeflowing style, many of the students and teachers who reacted to Susan's essay saw her as the type to change her personality to suit the social situation. One student described her this way:

> I think Susan is the type who has two personalities. I don't mean that in a negative way. She seems as though she is one person when she is with her parents and old friends, and someone else when she is at school. Despite the fact she preaches individualism is good, she clearly does not live by that standard.

This protean image, which Jung might call the archetype of transformation and rebirth, is often present in NF writing. It can be a powerful force when the NF is an advocate for change to an audience who wants change. But, if NFs seem to be forcing change on people who want stability, they may provoke a negative reaction from their audience.

It is important for NF writers to realize that any potential audience will go through periods when they want change and periods when they fear change. During those periods when change is needed and desired, NFs can powerfully use their preferred style to suggest new alternatives. When their audience wants stability, NFs might want to adopt another style to avoid alienating their audience.

Moving Beyond Your Natural Style

We believe that the concept of a natural style carries with it important consequences. If we have a natural style, does that mean that the way we write is predetermined? Does that mean that we can never develop as writers, learn new styles, or change our style to adapt to a particular audience?

The concept of a natural style might seem to suggest that how we write is fixed or predetermined. The opposite is actually closer to the truth. It is through understanding the way that our personality seems to emerge in our writing, even without our conscious control, that we learn how we can develop as writers. Understanding our natural style means understanding our strengths and weaknesses; it means understanding our starting point and where we need to travel. It does not mean resigning to our fate.

While all types can certainly alter their natural style of writing, the effects are often variable. We may, for example, change our style to please an audience and wind up making things worse. Or we might fail to change our style when we should have.

When the two of us were nearing completion of an earlier book we were writing together, George, an INTJ, asked John, an INFP, to write the preface. Here is the beginning of John's first draft:

> In the years that have passed since our initial drafts of this work were set to paper, the field of education has come alive with discussion of its proper mission and the proper means of accomplishing such a mission. As one example, Allan Bloom, in his provocative book *The Closing of the American Mind* (1978), proposes that universities once again should "encourage the noninstrumental use of reason for its own sake" (p. 249). One factor which Bloom believes to be behind the lost mission of the university is described by Saul Bellow in the foreword to Bloom's book. Bellow decries the fact that...

John's draft went on to cite other authorities on the role of literacy in American higher education. He was attempting to place the book that he and George had just finished into an academic context. He was also trying to speak to an audience of professional teachers of college composition. In order to try to reach this audience, John abandoned his natural style. As an NF, he would have preferred to tell a story about how the book was written.

When George read John's draft, he hated it. Even though he was one of those professionals who John was trying to reach, and even though his NT type preferences are consistent with a heavy majority of those faculty who might buy the book, he wrote back to John that a preface should provide a personalized background on how we came to write the book. George was, in part, reacting to John's rather forced attempt to reach an NT audience, but he also felt that this particular piece of writing, the preface, needed to be more personal and engaging. John then wrote the following, which became the beginning of the book's preface:

> It was during a lunchtime conversation more than eight years ago that the name of C. G. Jung first came up between us. At the time, George was curious about the content of a workshop that John, a university counseling center psychologist, was preparing. The workshop, designed to help students understand how personality differences influence their preferred learning styles, drew upon Jung's theory.... Several lunch discussions later, George, the coordinator of academic support services at the university, suggested that the theory might also shed light on how students approach writing. To find out, we generated some hypotheses and then began to test them in a weekly support group for graduate students.

As already mentioned, NF types like John lose their voice when they try to appeal to too many different readers or when they assume that certain types of readers will always want things worded in their own way.

Interestingly, the writing of this very chapter reflected a similar dilemma. George wrote the first draft and sent it to John with a note: "John, This is a *rough* draft. George." You may find it interesting to compare the following introduction to George's draft to what actually appears at the front of this chapter:

> That individuals have a kind of natural style, a way that seems related to their personality type, has been widely acknowledged for a long time. Aristotle used the word *ethos* to describe how the speaker's personality entered the speech and how that "character" in the text affected the audience's willingness to believe or doubt the speaker. Contemporary writing specialists often use to term *voice* to explain the presence of an author in writing; the metaphor suggests that the author, when he or she is writing well, breathes life into the text. In this book, we will call this "character" or "voice" that enters a text, at least those texts that seem distinctive or authentic, the writer's natural style. We believe, as we will show in this chapter, that type theory can add substance to the long-standing discussion of how the personality of the writer enters his or her text.

George's historical introduction to the concept of *ethos* reflects the natural interest of an NT writer. It also, of course, reflects George's chosen profession as a college professor in English. This particular book, written for a general audience, required a more informal style. So George revised his introduction to make it a little less academic, a little less NT.

Conclusion

As we mature as writers, we learn to adapt to different situations, which often means learning to write in new ways. We certainly cannot go through life with only one style and expect to be an effective writer in all situations. In the chapters that follow, we will discuss the development of a single piece through drafting and revising, our development as writers, and writing for different audiences. Those chapters should offer some suggestions on how to adopt, if only temporarily, the natural style of another type.

Drafting
and Revising

A knowledge of your personality type can suggest ways that you might best draft an essay and then revise it. First, however, we need to say something about drafting and revising. Because drafting an essay is usually the most difficult part of writing, we feel that it is important that as you are struggling to get your ideas onto paper, you write in whatever process comes most naturally. This means writing in a way that fits your personality type and draws on the strengths of your preferences.

Once you have finished a rough draft, once you have some basic ideas down on paper, you can begin to revise. Too often, writers view revision as a mechanical process of following some rather general rules—cut excess words, add some examples, check the spelling. Instead, we would like for you to think of revision literally as *revisioning*, or seeing again what you have already written. A revision might entail an entirely new approach—a new organizational strategy, reworking the style, or changing the central point of what you want to say. We would also like for you to think of revision as the time that you think about adapting what you have written for the specific audience that will be reading it.

It is easier to draft an essay when we write it our way—when we are, in effect, trying to explain our ideas to ourselves. Sometimes the way that we draft a piece of writing will also make sense to the people we want to read it. Then we may not have to revise it extensively. At other times, the way that we drafted the essay may be entirely inappropriate for our intended audience. Then we need to think about how to translate a rough draft into a new form or style. This is a more difficult revision process because now we must shift from writing for ourselves to writing for others.

While drafting and revising can be difficult processes, often leaving us feeling like we are lost in the wilderness, we will explain how you can use your newfound knowledge of your personality type as a road map. When you are feeling lost in a rough draft, you can think of your preferences and be reminded of natural strengths that can help you. When you are feeling disoriented about revision, you can think about what might be the personality type of your intended audience and shift to writing for that type of person.

Certainly, the kind of general advice on drafting and revising that we offer in this chapter is appropriate for some audiences and writing contexts and not for others. In this chapter, we will suggest how to round out your writing and how to make conversational writing more formal or formal writing more conversational. As a writer, you will need to decide which style is more appropriate for your setting and audience, a topic which we will take up in chapter 16.

Extraversion

The natural strengths of an Extravert include talking out ideas, thinking while doing, leaping into tasks, using trial and error to problem solve, and thinking quickly. We usually do not think of these strengths as ones that are easily applied to writing. But that is primarily because writing instruction was, for many years, dominated by Introverted teachers who taught students to write in an Introverted process. Many very successful professional writers have found ways to write in a more Extraverted fashion. The main thing that Extraverts need to think about is how they can make writing more like talking. Some ideas of how Extraverts can begin drafts and how they can revise follow.

Extraverted Ways to Begin Drafts
- Talk out your ideas first, seeking reactions from others.
- Dictate your thoughts and have someone else record them.
- Find out what you have to say by leaping into writing.
- Compose on a word processor so you can work by trial and error.

- Write in a more conversational style so you feel like you are talking to a close friend.
- Write in a noisy, stimulating environment so you don't feel like you are missing out on life.

Extraverted Ways to Revise

- Outline after writing a first draft as a means of improving organization and clarifying focus.
- Improve the focus by centering on a few ideas and developing them in more depth.
- Ask for feedback.
- Revise the introduction and early sections that might have been written before you figured out what you wanted to say.
- Cut redundant words and ideas.

When we listen to many of our greatest orators, we find that they repeat themselves for emphasis. Sometimes they even interrupt themselves as they speak. But if we read these speeches, they often do not come across half as well as they sounded. Oral and written communication follow different rules. One is based primarily on sound, the other on how words appear visually on the page. Thus, when they revise, Extraverts, who naturally like to write as if they were speaking, may need to translate their casual style into more formal language. Sometimes, a rather conversational style is better; it is usually easier to read and more friendly. At other times, say, when writing for a professional journal, a more formal style is required. In these cases, Extraverts will often need to revise their drafts to make them less conversational. Here are some ways to make your writing more formal.

Ways to Make Writing More Formal

- Cut "well," "so," and "then" when used as interjections, as in "Well, do you know what happened?"
- Cut intensifiers, especially "really" (as in a "really good time") and "pretty" (as in "pretty good").
- Cut slang, such as "cop" for "police officer."

- Replace general words, such as "something," "this," "someone," "get," and "put," with more specific words.
- Avoid abbreviations.

Extraverts often write quickly so that the act of writing can keep up with their rapid thought process. As a result, they may write sentences that ramble on, as their speech often does. The following sentence from an essay on advertising is an example:

Merchants also have celebrities and famous people on their commercials to help the product sell because a lot of viewers will purchase the product because their idol was on the commercial and the viewer truly believes they actually use the product they're advertising.

Such sentences may need to be broken up into several sentences. They can also be improved by cutting excess words, switching around the order of clauses, putting important words in the subject and verb positions, and adding qualifications and descriptive words. With these changes, notice how the sentence becomes more formal:

Merchants also hire celebrities, such as Chris Evert, Michael J. Fox, and Bill Cosby, to endorse their products and create extremely effective advertisements. If naive viewers are convinced that their idol, whom they believe to be beyond fault, actually trusts the product, they will probably buy it.

Extraverts should not be concerned about writing rough drafts in a conversational style; as we have suggested above, an informal rough draft can often be easily edited to suit a more formal audience if appropriate.

Introversion

While Extraverts need to make writing more like talking, Introverts usually need to find some quiet time to do their drafting. This does not mean that they will never benefit from talking about their ideas or hearing feedback on their rough drafts. However, when they are in the process of trying to fashion their thoughts into a rough draft, they tend to find talk from others an intrusion. Here are some introverted ways of beginning and revising rough drafts.

Introverted Ways to Begin Drafts

- Find a quiet place to concentrate on the first draft.
- Put your initial ideas on paper, at least in rough form.
- Work out a tentative outline of where the topic might go.
- Think about your writing while you are doing things alone, like exercising, cooking, driving, or mowing the lawn.

Introverted Ways to Revise

- Add personal examples that bring your ideas to life.
- Talk about your early drafts with someone you know.
- Ask others to respond to what you have on paper.
- Look for ways to add humor to your writing.

Some Introverts tell us that they write papers in their heads, even mentally revise and edit them, then just sit down and transcribe that mental text onto paper. As you might imagine, their rough drafts often seem more formal and polished than those of Extraverts. It might seem, especially to the Introvert, that little revision is needed. But Introverts sometimes need to write less formally. This book, for example, was written by two Introverts who wanted to write less formally than they usually do for professional journals. We tried to use some of the techniques below.

Ways to Make Writing More Conversational

- Insert "well," "so," or "then" as interjectives, such as "So, how do we handle this?"
- Address your audience directly as "you."
- Use fewer long, complex sentences.
- Use more common everyday words, not necessarily slang, but words that we would be more likely to hear in conversation.
- Begin some sentences with coordinating conjunctions ("So...").

Because Introverts prefer to be uninterrupted when they write, they may be reluctant to seek advice in their writing process. Even when they revise extensively, they may prefer to make the kinds of changes that they want to make, instead of reworking a manuscript to suit the views of others. They need to learn that they can often improve their writing enormously by hearing about possible revisions from close friends.

Sensing

Because they value "doing things the right way" and meeting the expectations of teachers or bosses, Sensing types write best when they have clear directions. If a teacher, for example, asks them to write a research paper on any topic or to write about something they feel is important, they will often feel lost. When blocked by vague directions, Sensing types need to ask for clarification. If their teacher or boss is unwilling or unable to clarify expectations, the Sensing type writer should ask fellow students or colleagues. Clear directions will help them get going.

Once they begin writing, Sensing types need to build on the tried and true. A model suggested by an authority can help. If they find a format that worked for them in the past, all the better. Sensing types do not want to reinvent the wheel.

And the facts come first. This grounds them in reality. They want to follow grammar and mechanics, which provide the kind of clear guidelines that they value, the kind of guidelines that are often missing from writing. Here are some ways Sensing types begin and revise their writing.

Sensing Ways to Begin Drafts

- Ask authorities what is required for this kind of writing.
- Put notes, references, and other resources within easy reach.
- Make a list of what has worked in the past and refer to it when blocked.
- Write first what you know for sure about the topic.
- Start with the facts.

Sensing Ways to Revise
- Look for themes in the concrete information you wrote.
- Write a brief statement for those themes.
- Put the theme summary at the beginning of your draft.
- Clearly show how your concrete data are examples of that central theme.
- Remove details that are already stated or implied.
- Make sure every paragraph states a central point and everything in that paragraph is related to that idea.

The revisions of Sensing types, however, must overcome what is lacking in their first drafts. This usually means that they need to find an overarching theme so that the reader can understand the importance of the data they present. Many readers may want to know this general theme right from the beginning. Sensing types can leave space for this thesis statement at the beginning of their paper, but they may not know what to write in that space until *after* they have carefully recorded all the facts about the topic. When revising, they may need to remove some—perhaps many—of their details, especially if these details do not relate to the theme that they have decided on.

Intuition

Intuitives usually want to find ways to make their writing unique. When given detailed, specific directions by a teacher or boss, they often ignore them so that they can find some original approach to the writing task. They may, as a result, ignore very useful, practical advice or write something that their teacher or boss will find unacceptable.

While it is facts and details that drive the rough drafts of Sensing types, it is ideas that get Intuitives going. The "big picture" is their inspiration, and the bigger the better, at least to get them going. Here are some ways for Intuitives to begin and revise drafts.

Intuitive Ways to Begin Drafts

- Ignore for now the requirements of the writing task.
- Come up with original, interesting ideas on the topic.
- Find themes or theories to connect these loose ideas.
- Look for a unique slant on the topic.
- Find an original way to organize your ideas.

Intuitive Ways to Revise

- Be sure each idea has some facts or examples to support it.
- Reread the draft carefully for mechanical errors.
- Change the draft to meet the formal requirements.
- Remove words, phrases, or paragraphs that don't relate.

When they revise, Intuitives need to become more practical. In many kinds of writing, especially in the business world, their grand ideas need grounding in reality, with facts to support them. A concrete fact or two can make the larger purpose of the paper even more inspiring. Adding in facts or details can also be a way of testing out or or clarifying ideas. Then the ideas of Intuitives will not seem so dreamy.

Thinking

Thinking types usually prefer an objective distance from their topics, especially as they begin to write. They need to present a rationale for what they are writing about, or at least have that rationale clearly in their minds. Their rough drafts may itemize a few key points in a simple list or use words that reflect the presence of logical thought: *if, then, however, due to, thus,* and *in conclusion.* Here are some ways for Thinking types to begin and revise drafts.

Thinking Ways to Begin Drafts

- Put your facts or ideas in logical order.
- Arrange pieces of information into categories.

- Get to the point.
- Support each argument with evidence.
- Point out the flaws in the arguments of others.

Thinking Ways to Revise

- Add personal examples and language (use "I," "you," and "we").
- Give credit where it is due; try to understand the position of others rather than argue with them.
- Qualify wording if readers might take offense.

When they revise, Thinking types often need to add the missing subjective factor: people and what they care about. Some projects especially require that they personalize their drafts. In those cases, they can use the first person to state opinions ("I believe...") or to relate personal anecdotes. Because they focus on the content rather than the audience when writing rough drafts, they may need to consider who their audience is and think of ways to respond to the audience's special needs, both in terms of what they say and how they say it.

Feeling

It is very hard for all people, but especially Feeling types, to write about topics that they do not find personally important. If given a required topic to write on, Feeling types must discover something about it that pertains, or could pertain, to their personal values or their most cherished and strongly held beliefs. Feeling types want to touch the lives of others. If a writing assignment seems to be a mere intellectual exercise, they will find it difficult. When forced to write on a topic they do not have a personal interest in, they need to try to give it a new slant, to take a perspective that will relate the topic to something they are in some way invested in.

It is probably a good idea for Feeling types to spend a little time making a list about what they believe, what they feel most strongly about, and what they most want to accomplish in their life. Then, when they are blocked by a difficult topic, they can look at the list and try to relate the topic to one of those values. Here are some ways for Feeling types to begin and revise drafts.

Feeling Ways to Begin Drafts

- Write on what you care about or what's important to you.
- Express your conviction and investment in the topic.
- Find words that will capture your reader's attention.
- Let your ideas flow naturally from one idea to the next.

Feeling Ways to Revise

- Get to the point, perhaps by shortening your sentences.
- Take out excessive references to what you value.
- Put your ideas into categories and then order them.
- Show how one fact or idea leads logically to another.

When writing revisions, especially for professional audiences, Feeling types may need to focus on toughening up their language, trying to get to the point in fewer words, and presenting criteria or "road signs" for the emerging direction of their thoughts. An argumentative style comes more naturally to Thinking types, but Feeling types will also express critiques and challenges if they know that this is what their readers, in this particular situation, expect. Feeling types can also argue more effectively if they think of the process less as criticizing someone else than as expressing their own opinions and beliefs.

Judging

Judging types do not like to keep options open any longer than necessary. They take charge of their writing project, narrow their topics, bring their research to a close, plan their time, and get the first draft completed. They get things done. Here are some ways for Judging types to begin and revise drafts.

Judging Ways to Begin Drafts

- Select a specific topic and put other options aside.
- Organize your schedule and plan times for writing in stages.
- Focus your first draft on the topic.
- Write conclusive statements.

Judging Ways to Revise

- Raise unanswered questions about the topic.
- Elaborate on statements with facts or new possibilities.
- Suggest ways to look at things that contradict your view.
- Expand on parts of your writing that may be too brief.
- Do more research to fill in the gaps.

The downside of the Judging types' approach to writing is that they need instead to neglect the virtues of withholding judgment for a while. They need instead to delay closure until more information is in. They can revise their first drafts by expanding them or presenting implications for further research. Their naturally confident way of presenting their topic can be enhanced further by stating forthrightly that not everything is known about certain aspects of it. They can look for places in their language to raise questions instead of mainly making pronouncements.

Perceiving

Perceiving is a process of noticing, looking, listening, and gathering information and ideas. Perceiving types, therefore, need to be as expansive and inclusive as they can when they begin. Numerous possible topics should be considered, and connections among them explored. Information from one topic can be found to relate in unexpected ways to another topic. First drafts can, and should, be long, including things that might later be found to be tangential. Narrowing and shortening are for later—as much later as possible. Here are some ways for Perceiving types to begin and revise drafts.

Perceiving Ways to Begin Drafts

- Keep topic options open even after you begin writing.
- Let the first draft be as long as you feel it needs to be, regardless of the page requirements.
- Delay coming to definitive conclusions until later.
- Look for interesting connections among your ideas.

Perceiving Ways to Revise

- Focus your topic, but as near to the deadline as possible.
- Shorten your sentences, paragraphs, and the entire paper.
- Finish with definite conclusions, even if you feel they are only tentative.
- Tell yourself that this draft is good enough, for now.

When the deadline really is just around the corner (usually tomorrow morning!), the time has arrived for a Perceiving type to omit or shorten long phrases, paragraphs, pages, or whole themes. Focus is needed. Conclusions must be presented, at least tentatively. "Given the present look at the evidence, one possible conclusion is…" can be a way for Perceiving types to get past feeling that they do not know enough to finish their writing. The written project is never fully in its final form, even though it has already been delivered to the teacher, the boss, or the publisher. It is, however, "good enough." For now.

Conclusion

In this chapter, we have explained, in general terms, how to write a rough draft in your own way and then revise it for your audience— the specific people to whom you are writing or the social context in which you write. Sometimes you may need to translate a rough draft into a final draft, almost as if you were translating a text from one language to another. The general advice in this chapter, as well as more specific advice that will come in later chapters, will provide some guidelines, but you may also need to analyze specific audiences and kinds of writing situations in more detail. You can begin to do this by thinking about what might be the personality type of your audience and then revising your rough draft to meet the needs of that type of person.

Growing
as a Writer

We never stop developing as writers. Even relatively experienced writers must recognize their natural starting point and then bring balance to their writing. Each of the preferred parts of our personality has both pitfalls and strengths. In this chapter, we will show how individuals of different type preferences tend to grow as writers.

The Writing Development
of Extraverts and Introverts

The table on the following page summarizes some of the writing strengths and limitations of Extraverts and Introverts, which are discussed below.

Extraverts: Interaction
Balanced With Reflection

Extraverts write best when they begin with their outer lived experience. They thus would rather talk and act than observe or record events on paper. And they should, as much as possible. That is why we recommended in earlier chapters that Extraverts talk into a tape recorder, invite a partner to bounce ideas around with them, or take breaks from too much quiet sit-alone activity. Computer word processing may work well for them when they interact with the screen, as if the computer is another person responding to their thoughts.

When Extraverts develop, they are able to shut off the outer world and turn their attention to serious matters. They not only can sit quietly to write, they may even prefer to. They are not turning into Introverts by doing so. Indeed, after periods of quiet writing, they need a

Writing Strengths and Limitations of Extraverted and Introverted Types	
Extraverted (E)	**Introverted (I)**
Physical proximity to topic and audience	*Physical distance from topic and audience*
Strengths: Extraverts excel at writing from experience. Their prose can be vital and reflect a clear connection between experience and thought. They tend to excel at writing dialogues from outer speech and usually have a clear sense of voice. At best, they write vital informal prose that reflects an immediacy of experience.	**Strengths:** Introverts tend to write more intensely about a more limited range of ideas or topics (especially if also Judging). They will usually reflect on their topic enough to make abstractions from it and clearly perceive the audience as having values different from their own. At best, they condense ideas into a naturally formal style.
Limitations: Extraverts may write more fragmentally, touching superficially on a broad range of topics (especially if also Perceiving). They may inadequately reflect on their topic or fail to differentiate their values from those of their audience (especially if also Thinking). At worst, they present undigested information in an inappropriate and conversational style.	**Limitations:** Introverted writing may be so distant from experience that it lacks vitality or fails to reflect clearly the connection between experience and thought. Intorverts may be reluctant to express ideas and feelings, even on paper. At worst, they produce a lifeless and needlessly formal prose (especially if also Thinking).

From *Personality and the Teaching of Composition* by George H. Jensen and John K. DiTiberio, pp. 98–99. Norwood, NJ: Ablex, 1989. Copyright 1989 by Ablex. Reprinted by permission from Ablex Publishing Corporation.

burst of intense movement, talk, activity at the office, or a rollicking party. When it came time for one ENFP we know to write the final draft of his dissertation, he checked himself into a hotel room, unplugged the television, disconnected the phone (except when he needed to call out for food), and wrote in solitude intensively for a week until it was done. He then took the draft to his adviser, went home to his wife and kids, and called his friends over to share a keg of beer.

The content of the mature writing of an Extravert retains its vitality and closeness to life. But it also begins to explore deeper issues and insights.

As they approach midlife, Extraverted writers may find themselves interested more and more in reflective writing. They often start journals or write about material that draws more on their Introversion.

Introverts: Reflection
Balanced With Interaction

Introverts write best when they begin with their long-considered thoughts about a topic. Especially as young writers, they prefer to sit quietly with a notepad or stare at a wall to gather inspiration. Novelist Edna Ferber reflects on the Introverted process in the following words:

> The ideal view for daily writing, hour on hour, is the blank wall of a cold-storage warehouse. Failing this, a stretch of sky will do, cloudless if possible.

When Introverts use a computer, they want the word processing program to be so familiar that there are no surprises. When problems do occur, it feels like an evil demon sits inside the computer interrupting their creative process. First drafts come best without interruptions. Intoverts tend to share their drafts with others only after going through them several times themselves.

In Stephen B. Oates' biography of Abraham Lincoln, he leads us to believe that Lincoln was an Introvert. Here is how he approached writing:

> Lincoln usually wrote at a table with two high windows sitting in a large armchair with his legs crossed. This June he worked on his message to Congress writing in his usually slow and laborious manner.... From time to time he would pause to stare out the windows.

As they mature, Introverted writers connect more regularly to the outer world. The accumulation of experience itself brings more of the outer world under consideration. Thus, the boundary is less firm between inside and out. It may look to others as if they have magically turned into Extraverts. They have not. Once they become familiar with another person, environment, or topic, Introverts can interact with them comfortably, because they now represent an outer extension of their inner rehearsed dialogue.

The content of the mature writing of an Introvert becomes increasingly vivid while less ponderous and distant. Real-life examples and illustrations will flavor the drafts without sacrificing their underlying depth and serious message.

As they approach midlife, Introverts become more interested in bringing their writing to wider audiences and putting into public the inner thoughts that have percolated for years. Ideas that were previously only shared with colleagues or in personal logs may now serve as the foundation for conducting a workshop or running for public office.

The Writing Development of Sensing and Intuitive Types

The table on the following page summarizes some of the writing strengths and limitations of Sensing and Intuitive types, which are discussed below.

Sensing Types: Realism Balanced With Imagination

Of the four functions, Sensing most consistently tends to work against students as they move from elementary to secondary to higher education in this country. Even Feeling, which is often not valued in education, appears to be less of a liability, as long as it is paired with Intuition rather than Sensing. Young writers who favor Sensing want to know for sure about a topic before reporting on it. To be sure means to slow down your perceptive process to look, listen, touch, smell, or taste.

Writing Strengths and Limitations of Sensing and Intuitive Types

---

Sensing (S)

Focus on concrete, sensory data

Strengths: Sensing types excel at following directions closely, attending to concrete observations, and accurately presenting data. At best, they write accurate descriptions and sound technical reports; they also tend to be proficient at dealing with complex data sets.

Limitations: Sensing types may fail to present the ideas and concepts behind their concrete data. They may fail to see the unique demands of the rhetorical situation and to adjust their writing to meet those demands. At worst, they present mere facts in a hackneyed formula.

Intuitive (N)

Focus on generalities, implications, inferences, and possibilities

Strengths: Intuitive types excel at developing unique approaches to a topic. At best, they write imaginatively and originally about sound concepts and theories.

Limitations: Intuitives may leap into the middle of the piece and fail to provide background information. They may fail to include support (examples, facts, etc.) for ideas and may find it difficult to follow directions. At worst, their writing is incomprehensively abstract and complex, based on flighty, inaccurate hunches.

As students progress from elementary to secondary to college education, they find fewer Sensing teachers who are patient with their slow-but-sure method of learning and writing. Their Intuitive instructors instead value flashes of insight, quick leaps, hypotheses, and originality. The writing of young Sensing types is therefore often labeled as "merely concrete." When one of us was writing a textbook for classroom use, he wanted to include some assignments such as summarizing, which Sensing types generally like and are often good at. The academic textbook reviewers (who tend to be Intuitives) hated these assignments, saying they were too easy, too low-level. The author argued back that summarizing was a skill, one that was actually difficult for many students and needed to be taught, but they wouldn't buy it. The assignments never appeared in the published text.

Especially when anxious, Sensing writers employ a building-block approach in order to see how the bits and pieces fit together. Gradually, they are able to see the broader patterns. They then review the sequence to notice themes that characterize clusters of their facts. One or two of these themes can serve as the thesis of the paper. Intuitive instructors tend to want this thesis statement near the beginning of the paper.

Intuitives might describe the theme-building process as simplifying, since they find facts and data by themselves to be baffling and uninspiring. But simplicity to a Sensing type is in the facts alone. If writing about apples, they feel grounded in reality to know, for example, how many were available, what color each was, and what each felt, smelled, tasted, looked, and sounded like as they ate them. This process is similar to that recommended by E. D. Hirsh, whose books have become popular for proposing that we teach basic facts to students. In *Cultural Literacy: What Every American Needs to Know,* his comments about writing speak to the natural gifts of Sensing types:

> Reading and writing are cumulative skills; the more we read the more necessary knowledge we gain for further reading....

Accumulating facts is what Sensing types like to do. Unfortunately, much of what Hirsh has to say is designed to sort out what he thinks are good methods from bad ones. The accumulation of facts, in his view, distinguishes literate children from illiterate ones.

In contrast, mature Sensing writers retain their preference for reality—for getting their facts straight. But from these preferred beginnings, their writing becomes increasingly imaginative and conceptually original. Most importantly, experience is their best teacher.

With practice, they will master the skills of conceptualizing and brainstorming. They are no less imaginative than Intuitives, but they tend to trust their imagination only when it has boundaries around it, for example, by writing a mystery novel from a formula. Persistence and perspiration, the natural virtues of Sensing types (especially SJs), can teach them behaviors that come more naturally to Intuitives.

Intuitive Types: Imagination Balanced With Realism

Intuition is increasingly valued as students progress through school and into college. Young Intuitives write more easily if the activity inspires their imagination, which is boundless. The wildest fantasy of a young child, if trusted and nurtured, lays the groundwork for mature originality. Open associations to a word may lead, for example, to a discovery about how the word has been used in fascinating ways in the history of language.

The danger, of course, is that immature Intuition can be so loose that the writing results are meaningless. As with all aspects of writing, the distinction must be made between process and product. Brainstorming, by definition, must not be too focused, evaluated, or organized. These creative juices, however, must be refined if they are to be productive.

The South American novelist Gabriel Garcia Marquez was asked if he works very differently now than when he was young. His reply sounds like that of a seasoned Intuitive type:

> The writing process is very different. When you are young, you write almost like writing a poem. You write on impulses and inspiration. You have so much inspiration that you are not concerned with technique. You just see what comes out, without worrying much about what you are going to say and how.... When you are older, when the inspiration diminishes, you depend more on technique. If you don't have that, everything collapses. There is no question that you write much more slowly, with much more care, and perhaps with less inspiration.

As they mature, Intuitive writers continue to trust their global impressions and their imagination. But they then move toward making their ideas more understandable to a general reader. They simplify their language without losing the meaning of their message. They provide real-life illustrations to represent the theory they espouse. They produce facts to support their hypotheses. Explicit communication becomes possible (as in an instructional manual) without sacrificing their natural gift for subtle expression and implication (as in an inspirational sermon).

Ernest Hemingway's writing was known for its straightforward style. His words were crafted so carefully, however, that their simplicity was deceiving. In *The Garden of Eden,* Hemingway's main character was a writer named David Bourne. As seen in the section below, Bourne's advice to himself reflects Hemingway's own growth as a writer:

> Be careful, he said to himself. It is all very well for you to write simply and the simpler the better. But do not start to think so damned simply. Know how complicated it is and then state it simply.

For Hemingway, simple wordings were developed in the service of complex ideas, rather than for their own sake.

The Writing Development of Thinking and Feeling Types

The table on the following page summarizes some of the writing strengths and limitations of Thinking and Feeling types, which are described below.

Thinking Types: Objective Analysis Balanced With Personal Investment

Young Thinking types like reasons for doing things, including writing. They do not yet have the language or cognitive development to articulate a rationale or establish logical criteria for their

---

Writing Strengths and Limitations of Thinking and Feeling Types

---

Thinking (T)	Feeling (F)
Emotional distance from topic and audience	*Emotional proximity to topic and audience*
Strengths: Thinking types excel at the logical development of essays. They tend to write objectively and analytically. At best, they will present content clearly and develop sound and consistent organizational patterns.	**Strengths:** Feeling types excel at using personal examples, writing expressively, making contact with the audience, and conveying the deep personal conviction behind their beliefs. At best, they produce stylish, interesting, and personal prose.
Limitations: Thinking types may regard their beliefs as universally held (especially if also Extraverted) and thus write abrasively or dogmatically. They may objectify ideas and examples until they lose personal appeal. Their organizational patterns may be too structured—a narrative may read like a technical report. At worst, they may, by writing abrasively or dryly, fail to connect with their audience.	**Limitations:** The writing of Feeling types may be gushy or overly sentimental. They often dislike analyses or making critical remarks and may, out of concern for others' feelings, soften criticism until it is unclear or lacks force. Their organization may be so free-flowing that their thoughts seem contradictory (especially if also Extraverted). At worst, they write sentimentally and unclearly.

From *Personality and the Teaching of Composition* by George H. Jensen and John K. DiTiberio, pp. 98–98. Norwood, NJ: Ablex, 1989. Copyright 1989 by Ablex. Reprinted by permission from Ablex Publishing Corporation.

decisions. This comes later. But they ask for explanations and expect answers.

When they write, young Thinking types likewise produce rudimentary categories for things and people. They might, at their worst, be accused of treating people as if they were things. (Conversely, immature Feeling types sometimes treat things as if they were people). If writing about American presidents, for example, young Thinking types may classifiy them as basic as Republicans versus Democrats, those who had served in the military versus those who had not, and one-term presidents versus those who served longer. Thinking types are interested in how things work, being competent, and being able to explain what they are doing.

The writing of young Thinking types is informative but often blunt. It may neglect the needs of the reader. It also often fails to communicate what the writer actually cares about. The Thinking type tends to take for granted that simply because they are writing about a topic, the audience will know that they are interested in it. With maturity, Thinking types see good reasons for building a relationship with their audience—it may make them want to read the next page.

Former president John F. Kennedy reflected on how he could develop his speechwriting in the following comment:

> I think I'm primarily rational more than emotional.
> I need more emotion in my speeches. But at least I've got
> a control over the subject matter.

Jung himself wrote volumes over the course of his career. He identified himself as a Thinking and Intuitive type. Much of his writing was brilliant, but also emotionally distant and quite abstract. It wasn't until midlife, however, that he wrote on his theory of types, which many find the most personalized (Feeling) and practical (Sensing) of his writing.

Feeling Types: Personal Investment
Balanced With Objective Analysis

If young Feeling types are asked to write about American presidents, they will often start first with what they like or dislike about them—this one was admired by the public; another was an underdog who overcame adversity to get elected. Classifying leaves them cold, unless someone they feel close to asks them to do so. When they trust personal values as their best source of decision making, they have a sense of order in their lives that serves them well.

Nevertheless, in writing, the language of young Feeling types is very different from that of Thinking types. They express first what they care about—liking (or not) the main character in a story; being interested (or not) in the field trip they just attended. Even as very young students, they are mindful of who will read what they write. They seek to please and often accurately notice what even a Thinking type teacher wants of them in their writing assignments. At their worst, however, their writing can be overly sentimental or deficient in analysis. Maya Angelou is one of the most revered African American writers. In *I Know Why the Caged Bird Sings*, she wrote:

> I was well known for being "tender-hearted." Southern Negroes used that term to mean sensitive and tended to look upon a person with that affliction as being a little sick or in delicate health. So I was not so much forgiven as I was understood.

As they develop, Feeling type writers build upon their personal investment in a writing topic. This gives them energy and motivation to continue writing through the more careful categorization of the findings (as in a science project) or a listing of the pros and cons of an argument (as in a compare/contrast essay). They then recognize, as a Thinking type tends to do naturally, that they do not have to describe every value they hold, leaving some of them instead to be assumed.

The appropriate balance between objective reporting and personalization is defined differently by different writers. For example, John McPhee writes nonfiction essays on the natural world. In a talk to a convention of writing teachers, he once stated:

> If I need to be in my text I will. Otherwise I won't prance around.

The Writing Development of Judging and Perceiving Types

The table on the following page summarizes some of the writing strengths and limitations of Judging and Perceiving types, which are discussed below.

Writing Strengths and Limitations of Judging and Perceiving Types

---

Judging (J)

Exclusion of data and ideas to enhance decisiveness

Strengths: Judging types tend to be decisive and to reach conclusions quickly and thus forcefully assert a proposition. They tend to write quickly and to meet deadlines, and they may complete more projects than Perceiving types. At best, they write expediently and emphatically.

Limitations: In their haste to meet deadlines, Judging types are in danger of reaching premature closure. Their conclusions may be ill-considered or arbitrary. At worst, their writing can be opinionated, unambitious, and underdeveloped, and their statements can be unqualified.

Perceiving (P)

Inclusion of data and ideas to enhance thoroughness

Strengths: Perceiving types tend to investigate their topic thoroughly and present carefully considered ideas. Their writing tends to be fully developed and their ideas well supported. At best, they are thorough and present well-qualified conclusions.

Limitations: Perceiving types may be overinclusive and write on topics that are too broad. Their writing may be so thorough that it is tediously long, or it may be rife with digressions. They may be reluctant to assume a position in persuasive essays, open-endedly discussing both sides of the issue. At worst, their writing may seem to ramble endlessly without clear focus.

From *Personality and the Teaching of Composition* by George H. Jensen and John K. DiTiberio, pp. 98–99. Norwood, NJ: Ablex, 1989. Copyright 1989 by Ablex. Reprinted by permission from Ablex Publishing Corporation.

Judging Types: Decisiveness Balanced With Inclusiveness

Judging type writers appear mature, even as young children. The standard in most schools goes something like this: decide, get organized, work steadily, and get it done. The predominance of Judging type teachers in our schools (between sixty-five and seventy-five percent at all levels, kindergarten through university) tends to lead American educators to overlook the pitfalls of Judging type writers as well as the potential strengths of Perceiving types.

Immature use of Judgment in writing can produce foreclosure on a topic, finished drafts that are not backed by enough research, a rigidity of style, or a lack of openness to revision. As they mature, however, Judging types, while retaining their preference for decisiveness, plan into their schedules some time for flexibility. They learn, often from painful experience, that last-minute ideas and information can enrich their drafts. When they "plan for spontaneity," they schedule a cushion of open time during which they either reread what they have written, seek input from others, or integrate new material. They learn to flesh out their points or include perspectives that may not square a hundred percent with their main thrust but may put it into context. Their final drafts thus become less likely to sound as if they have found the final truth once and for all.

Perceiving Types: Inclusiveness Balanced With Decisiveness

In her recent book entitled *The Developing Child,* Elizabeth Murphy notes that Judging types plan from the present forward but Perceiving types plan from the deadline backward. Both are planful in their own way. But Perceiving types appear to a Judging type observer to be disorganized and indecisive, especially in the early stages of writing. Judging type teachers often assume that Perceiving type students are not taking the course seriously.

Immature Perceiving types can indeed be scattered, unfocused, and irresponsible. Although they resist too much structure—"Don't fence me in!"—they may need a deadline to be set by others. This allows them to know that all the possibilities will eventually be narrowed and to accept that their material is good enough, at least for now. They naturally look to the outer world to perceive all the interesting things there are to know or experience there. They likewise look outward to see when the world really requires a finished product.

The writing development of Perceiving types is thus a movement from inclusiveness to decisiveness. They make more definitive statements and do this with fewer words. They become more focused, organized, and responsible as they mature. They do not, however, abandon their need for openness and flexibility. They simply learn to trust their need to include all possible angles on the topic. This gives them energy to expend later on getting the draft finished at the very moment it is due.

Conclusion

In this chapter we have attempted to show how our growth as writers can coincide with our development as people. The general model suggests that we best work from strengths, from developing the use of our natural preferences first before attempting to make regular use of the contrasting processes. With the increased energy that comes from a familiar process, we can then achieve balance by turning attention to the neglected one. Younger writers will be generally less successful than older ones at this development, since they have not yet found their niche in a career or a commitment to a cause or relationship. Once balance among the various aspects of personality is achieved, writers can more comfortably make use of Sensing or Intuition, Thinking or Feeling, and all of the psychological processes as they write.

Getting Past Anxiety and Writer's Blocks

In this chapter, we will suggest how knowledge of your personality type can help you overcome writing anxiety or writer's blocks. *Writing anxiety* is a general stress—or distress—reaction to writing that leads to an avoidance of writing in general or to some specific type of writing. Regardless of ability, anyone who has had generally bad experiences with writing in the past can develop writing anxiety. Many people, however, do not. These people have had generally good experiences with writing, have a positive self-concept as a writer, and enjoy the challenge of tackling a new writing project.

Yet even those people who have generally good writing experiences sometimes find themselves staring at a blank sheet of paper or an empty computer screen. This is what is called *writer's block*.

To experience a writer's block means that on a specific writing project, our ability to make decisions about how to proceed has broken down—we simply do not know how to get started, what to write next, or which word to choose.

Personality and Writing Anxiety

Writers usually feel less anxiety about writing when they write in their own natural way. In fact, we have found that writers can often end paralyzing attacks of writing anxiety by learning to write in a way that is more suited to their personality. When Extraverts have been taught to write in isolation, make outlines, and produce a first draft that is a finished product, they usually experience anxiety. If they learn to freewrite or bring "talk" into their writing process, they generally feel much more comfortable about writing.

But this is not always the case. Sometimes, especially when we are under a lot of stress, we tend to exaggerate our preferences. Extraverts, for example, may start to talk rapidly, bouncing from idea to idea, spinning their wheels, unable to find a focus. In contrast, Introverts may plan obsessively, writing every word in their heads, even visualizing how each part of the text would look on paper, and then revising and editing this mental text. Both of these exaggerated processes lead to the same problem—the writer never puts any words down on paper. When this happens, writers need to try to find a balance. Extraverts need to write a little more like Introverts, and Introverts need to write a little more like Extraverts.

The following sections present some exercises for you to try if you are having problems with writing anxiety.

The Mapping Exercise

Extraverts can begin to be a little more Introverted in their writing process by doing some planning. While planning does not come naturally to Extraverts, they sometimes find it useful to jot some basic ideas down on a sheet of paper. This can help them focus their thoughts; they can even cross out those ideas that seem less important until they have arrived at a central idea that they can focus on for that particular piece of writing.

Whether you are an Extravert or an Introvert, try the following exercise. Select a topic for a brief essay and then *map out* the topic. In order to map out an idea, write it in the center of a sheet of paper and then circle it. Then write supporting ideas that are related to that secondary topic. Keep adding more and more details until you have the page filled up. See the example on the next page to help you get started.

Mapping not only helps Extraverts explore their ideas on paper, which can help them to get a better hold on those ideas, it can also help them narrow their topic. If they write about everything that they have mapped, the paper will usually be too broad. To narrow or focus the topic, begin to move out from the center until you find a supporting topic that seems more manageable.

Mapping Exercise

The Freewriting Exercise

When Introverts plan too much, they run into several kinds of problems. They may become stuck in the complexity of their plans, find writing (as in putting words on paper) a boring kind of transcription, or leave out so much of their thought process once they do put words on paper that their writing is underdeveloped or incomprehensible. If your writing process becomes too Introverted, you can play around with freewriting. Or you could learn to compose on a word processor, which seems to encourage Introverts to begin writing earlier, be more open to discovering ideas as they write, and view a first draft as being less permanent.

Here's an example of how to practice freewriting. With either a word processor or a notebook and pen, begin to type or write words and phrases—*any* words and phrases—onto the screen or paper. The phrases do not have to be grammatically correct—indeed, it is best if they are not. Let one line suggest another, like free association. When you get stuck, let your next words be about what it's like being stuck.

Freewriting Example

For hours I've stared at this notepad trying to figure what my next article is going to be like. I really wanted to write about the mess Clinton is in with all the new revelations about his personal life. But I don't know where to start. Sometimes I want to talk about the press and their insatiable nosiness. But I don't want to turn off these readers who—oh, forget it. I get too obsessed with how people feel about my position. I need to go ahead and say what's on my mind. Fact is, like it or not, what's important is that a vital young presidency is being derailed by political commentators who seem fearful of the very fact that youth is in the White House for a change—that the baby boom generation holds the reins of power.

With freewriting, the Introvert's serious deliberation is temporarily put aside so that the writer interacts with his or her multiple thoughts in a more lively way—a process that comes naturally to Extraverts when they talk. The inner censor is removed. Thus, the "garbage" and the "good stuff" both come out. After a page or two, or sometimes even only a few sentences, the writer may find a line or a phrase that can serve as the focus of his or her writing.

Personality and Writer's Blocks

Although some writers say that they do not experience writing anxiety, we have never talked to a writer who did not occasionally experience a writer's block. Writer's blocks seem to develop from a number of sources, but they, like writing anxiety, can quite often be traced back to our becoming locked into one approach, strategy, or technique. We may be using a way of writing that is either an exaggerated, unbalanced use of one of our preferences or a failure to use, when appropriate, an unpreferred process. For example, Introverts may be planning to an extreme and want every word written in their heads before even beginning to put words on paper. This would be using Introversion in an exaggerated way. Or an Introvert may be rigidly attempting to write like an Introvert in a situation that is more suited to an Extraverted approach. The key to overcoming many writer's blocks is learning to be more flexible and to draw upon our entire personality to help us get past difficult points in our writing process.

In what follows, we will explain how you can use knowledge of your personality type to diagnose the source of writer's blocks and adopt alternative writing strategies to move past them.

Extraversion

When we think of writer's blocks, we typically think of writing that does not happen; we conjure up the image of a writer staring at a blank page or a blank computer screen. The most common block that Extraverts experience is quite different. Extraverts can be writing frantically, filling pages of writing, but still be going nowhere. Their thoughts can come so quickly that they have trouble getting a handle on them—in other words, they are spinning their wheels.

When the writing process that tends to work best for Extraverts—such as quickly throwing words down on paper—begins to backfire, and they begin to spin their wheels, they can switch to another strategy. They can talk to a trusted friend or colleague or simply walk away from the writing for a while to give their unconscious mind a chance to reflect on what it wants to say.

If you are having trouble getting a handle on your ideas through writing, try talking to a friend to bring some clarity to your thoughts. We have found that this generally works better when the friend or colleague is an Introvert. The best way to proceed is to ask the friend to listen and write down whatever he or she considers to be a good idea. Once you have finished talking about what you want to write, give the friend some time to think about what has been said. Then ask him or her to give you a synopsis as well as the written list of good ideas. When you return to writing, you should have a greater sense of clarity and be able to produce writing that is going somewhere.

The opposite approach, to stop writing for a while, might seem more suited to Introverts—and it is. However, according to Carl Jung, our unconscious mind functions in the opposite way of our conscious mind. This means that the unconscious mind of an Extravert functions more like the conscious mind of an Introvert. While the conscious mind of an Extravert might thrive on trial and error, such as writing one's way into understanding what one wants to say, his or her unconscious mind is more likely to reflect on ideas. This is why Extraverts don't have the feeling that they think out their ideas. Instead, their ideas seem to happen to them, to come out of nowhere and magically appear.

When Extraverts tend to struggle with a piece of writing at the conscious level, by writing and writing and writing, they have a tendency to divert all of their energy to their conscious mind. If they walk away from a writing project when they are spinning their wheels, their unconscious mind will have a chance to reflect, clarify ideas, and then "suggest" a way to get writing working again. How is it that the unconscious mind can make suggestions to the conscious mind? We don't really know how this happens, but we can say when it happens. It is more likely to happen when the Extravert is either doing something actively, such as cooking or exercising, or is in a state of deep relaxation, for example, soaking in a hot bath, lying in bed, or meditating. So, the advice here is to relax and let it happen.

Introversion

Introverts generally feel the most comfortable with writing when they spend a great deal of time thinking about what they want to say and how they want to say it before beginning to put words to paper. When Introverts push this natural process to an extreme, however, they can become blocked. They may expect every idea to be perfectly clear and thoroughly considered. They may also attempt to write, revise, and edit a text before they transcribe it onto paper or into a word processor. In these cases, their text may never appear—it will remain something hidden away in their heads.

Introverts can overcome this block by writing more like Extraverts. They can try freewriting a rough draft by throwing any and every idea that pops into their heads onto a sheet of paper. Freewriting, the approach to writing that is more naturally an Extraverted process, can not only help Introverts to overcome specific writing blocks, it can also provide them with an important opportunity to develop as writers.

Even if Introverts only play with freewriting on occasion, this practice with writing by trial and error can help them understand that writing does not have to be completely planned out and written in one's head before a single word is put onto paper. All writers, including Introverts, need to understand that they can discover what they want to say, at least in part, while they are in the process of writing— that is, by putting words on paper. Once Introverts learn this and become open to discovering ideas while in the process of writing, they will be less obsessive about planning and crafting mental texts.

Just as an Extravert's unconscious mind is more reflective (the opposite of his or her conscious mind), so an Introvert's unconscious mind works by trial and error, more like the conscious world of an

Extravert. By freewriting, an Introvert is tapping into his or her unconscious mind, which is crucial if one is to overcome blocks. The unconscious mind often provides solutions to problems that the conscious mind cannot work out.

Sensing

Sensing types approach their writing like a craft. They tend to adopt, practice, and perfect an approach to writing such as a process, a series of techniques, or an organizational pattern, and then stick to it. As long as it works, they generally feel no need to develop a new approach. Although their crafting approach is very practical, it does have one drawback. Because they stick to one approach, they do not develop as wide a repertoire as Intuitive types. Thus, when they are faced with a new rhetorical context, one that places unique demands on them, they might attempt to force the old tried-and-true approach when it is inappropriate.

There is no quick and easy solution to this problem. But Sensing types certainly need to be encouraged to try new approaches and expand their repertoire so that they can be more adaptable to new situations in the future.

Beyond this, Sensing types are also a little more likely than Intuitive types to develop what writing analyst Mike Rose calls a *rigid rule*. A rigid rule is a belief that writing must always fulfill certain criteria. Some examples of rigid rules would be: A good writer never uses "I"; A good writer must have an interesting introduction; or A good writer must state the thesis as the last sentence of the first paragraph. Sometimes teachers who are unaware of the complexity of writing will instill such rules. But, in our experience, we have noticed that Sensing types can sometimes develop such rules on their own. They tend to view writing as a rule-governed procedure rather than an art. Sensing types need to be encouraged to view the standards of writing as part of an evolving art, as ultimately arbitrary matters of taste that constantly change. Good writers are people who at one time or another will break all of the rules about good writing.

A final block that sensing types encounter relates to their need for explicit directions. Sensing types like to fulfill the expectations of the teacher or the boss who gives them the writing assignment. When these directions are vague and unclear, Sensing types can feel like they have been set adrift. They need to learn, when they feel like they are a little lost, to ask their teacher or their boss to clarify the directions. If they have an Intuitive teacher or boss, Sensing types might expect to experience some frustration when a clarified instruction is just as vague as the original one. But in the long run, it will be easier to ask for more specific directions.

Intuition

One of the greatest strengths of Intuitive types is their originality, and it can also be their greatest failing. They sometimes become blocked because they cannot think of a unique approach. When attempting to write a poem, it makes sense to struggle with developing an original slant. But when writing a common everyday memorandum, struggling to be unique borders on the absurd. Yet, this is exactly what Intuitive types feel compelled to do.

Intuitive types can move past this block by trying to function more like Sensing types. They can think of an approach that worked in the past and try it again, even if it means giving up some originality. Or, they can simply focus on saying what they have to say without any frills. They can use what engineers like to refer to as the KISS method: *Keep it simple, stupid!* Not all writing has to be unique. Certainly, simple memoranda can be written very effectively and efficiently if the writer is willing to follow an established organizational pattern and just get the message across as simply as possible.

Thinking

Thinking types tend to excel at objective analysis. They are, thus, more likely to experience writer's block when they have to write on personal topics, which they tend to disdain as being too "touchy-feely."

Because they value being treated fairly, Thinking types might have difficulty writing in situations that they feel do not reward them for their efforts. When the situation does not seem to operate according to their notion of logical rules of order, they might simply have difficulty getting started.

Finally, Thinking types might encounter a block when they are unable to develop an acceptable organizational pattern. The structure of an organizational pattern—whether it be an outline, a model, or a general sense of what parts will go where—helps thinking types to think. Without such a structure, they may have difficulty making organizational decisions, deciding what should be included or excluded, or even developing their ideas.

Feeling

Feeling types generally feel most comfortable when they can write personally about a topic without having to follow a rigidly prescribed organizational pattern. To write personally about a topic does not mean that they must always write about events in their lives; it might simply mean that they take a personal approach to the topic, an approach that has people and personal values at its center. When they are forced to write more objectively and analytically, Feeling types may have difficulty motivating themselves to begin.

Whenever Feeling types begin a major writing project, they can spend some time writing—in a very personal way—about why completing the project is important to them and to their beliefs, values, and personal goals. This prelude of personal writing can make the real writing—the writing that must be done for a boss or teacher—easier to face.

Because Feeling types are very connected to their audience as they write, they might also experience blocks when they must write critically of another writer's work—even if they know that person will never read what they have written. The idea of criticizing someone else's work often conflicts with a Feeling type's need for harmony in personal relations. They can sometimes write what will usually pass as criticism more easily if they think in terms of writing their "opinions." For most feeling types, expressing personal "opinions" does not seem as harsh as "criticizing."

The need of Feeling types to connect with their audience can lead to much concern about word choice. This concern can be a strength, especially when producing such writing as poetic prose, but it can also lead to blocks in ordinary writing when they just cannot find the right word. To avoid this kind of block, Feeling types can learn to simply put down the best word that they can select at the moment. They can follow it with a question mark or even some alternative words within parentheses and then go back and think about the word in a later draft.

Judging

Judging types, who have a natural drive to push writing projects through to completion, might seem to be the types of writers who never or seldom experience writer's blocks. Yet their very drive to complete projects on time is precisely what leads to blocks. Judging types often force themselves to begin writing before they have done enough research or before they have let their ideas percolate long enough. Judging types need to learn to monitor and get a sense of their readiness to write. If they sit down to write and nothing happens or the writing is a struggle, then they need to reassess the situation. They need to decide whether they should do more research, spend more time talking out their ideas, or simply walk away from the writing and think about what they want to say for a few more days. In the following passage, writing specialist Donald Murray challenges the notion held by many teachers and writers that any resistance to writing is evil. On the contrary he feels it is a necessity that there be

> time for the seed of the idea to be nurtured in the mind. Far better writers than I have felt the same way. Over his writing desk Franz Kafka had one word, "wait." William Wordsworth talked of the writer's "wise passiveness"....
> Even the most productive writers are expert dawdlers.

Judging types also like to make a plan for completing their writing assignments. These plans can be rather complicated—much more than a simple schedule or a series of interim deadlines. They will not only think about the components of the writing project—the research, the drafts, the editing, and so on—and when each of these components needs to be completed, but they will also think about everything else that they must do, both at work and at home, and schedule these activities so that they do not interfere with completing the writing project. Once this plan is made, judging types tend to follow it—but sometimes they follow it too rigidly. They assume that the plan will work out. They assume that if they keep to the schedule and meet all of their interim deadlines, the final product will not only be done on time but will also be satisfactory. But the best made plans do not always work out. What Judging types need to learn to do is "plan to be spontaneous." They need to plan to stop at key points in their schedule and evaluate their progress, think about whether or not things are working out, and, if need be, revise their schedule.

Perceiving

Perceiving types, who generally delay closure until the last minute, might seem to live a life of writer's blocks. To others, they might seem to be chronic procrastinators who do not seem to take deadlines very seriously. To a certain extent this is true, but Perceiving types are usually very good at writing under pressure and pulling together a fairly decent text at the last minute. They write so frequently at the last minute that they develop what others call procrastination into an art form.

What is more likely to cause serious problems for Perceiving types is their tendency to overcommit themselves. Because they regard a deadline as something that can always be pushed back, they often say yes to new projects before they think about everything else they have to do. Soon, they find themselves working on more projects than any human could complete. Perceiving types also tend to try to work on many projects at once, doing a little on this one and then a little on that one. This means that they can work at a furious pace and finish nothing. The key here is to learn to say no.

Because Perceiving types like to be thorough, they sometimes fail to limit the scope of their writing projects. They conceive of dissertation topics that will take three years to complete, novels that will take twenty years to write, or research projects that will consume a lifetime. If they have the stamina to complete these projects, they will have an excellent finished project. But, too often, these enormous projects are never finished, especially if the Perceiving type lays one enormous project on top of another. Quite often Perceiving types can rely on friends who are Judging types to help them evaluate the scope of their projects and, if necessary, limit them.

Dealing With Writer's Blocks

As we have already mentioned, the first step in dealing with a writer's block is to figure out what is causing it. Not all writer's blocks will be related to your personality type, but we have found that many of them are. If you have knowledge of your personality type and the kinds of blocks that your type tends to encounter, then you can more quickly diagnose the cause of the block. Knowing why you are blocked is half the battle of getting past it.

The blocks that are associated with personality type often occur when our natural way of writing is out of balance—when we have taken a strength and pushed it to an extreme. The block can often be overcome by bringing some balance back into the process, either by being less extreme or by drawing on some unpreferred process. For example, an Intuitive type who is blocked because she is attempting to find a unique way of writing a simple memorandum can try to write it the way a Sensing type would. Then she can concentrate on clearly presenting the facts in a standard format.

Your reaction might be, Easier said than done. But Carl Jung said that our use of preferences is automatic; whereas, when we want to use our unpreferred functions, we have to think about it. So, we can be more flexible—we can use our unpreferred functions—if we simply "think about it." We find ourselves in the middle of writer's blocks because we tend to go through writing projects—indeed, we tend to go through life—without thinking about the best way to tackle a particular project. Again, knowledge of our personality type can help us to see more possibilities and alternative solutions to very common problems that we typically overlook because we are operating on autopilot.

Of course, sometimes we need a little help at getting to our unpreferred processes. When we cannot access them by simply thinking about using them, we can call them up in the service of one of our preferences. For example, Extraverted Sensing types can sometimes talk themselves into being more Intuitive. That is, through their natural strength of talking, or actively processing information, they can gain more access to their Intuition. And this might help them to get past a block.

One of the themes we have tried to develop in this chapter is that effective writers can build bridges between their conscious and unconscious worlds. In doing so, they are *not* making the unconscious mind fully conscious. Jung believed instead that we can become aware that a hidden world exists, but we must allow this unconscious world to speak its own indirect messages in its own way. That is why it is sometimes helpful, when Introverts are lost in concentration, simply to put the writing project aside and go do anything else to distract their attention—turn on a video, clean the basement, make some popcorn. When returning to the draft, sometimes their minds are more ready—in what may seem to be an almost magical way—just because they shifted their focus outward. Similarly, when Extraverts have been caught up in excessive talk or physical activity surrounding a project, they can benefit from shutting the door, unplugging the phone, turning off the radio or television, and focusing on one single idea at a time with a notepad in hand. This temporary, and often brief, shift in focus allows the preferred process to operate more clearly once the writer returns to it.

Conclusion

To summarize, we are suggesting two general rules for overcoming writing anxiety or blocks. First, learn to write in your natural way. If you are an Extravert, try writing more like an Extravert; if you are an

Introvert, learn to write using more of an Introverted process. Second, when your natural process is not working, look for some way to achieve some balance.

Writing for
Different Audiences

Most of us can remember how frustrating it was to try to figure out what different teachers wanted. We may have earned *A*s and *B*s in our English class one semester, but found ourselves writing *C* or *D* papers for a different teacher in the next. Each teacher seemed to want something different. But exactly what they wanted was often a mystery.

Unfortunately, the problem does not go away when we enter the world of work. Instead of trying to figure out what the teacher wants, we now struggle to figure out what the boss wants, what the customer wants, or what the client wants. We know that people have different tastes in writing, but determining which person prefers which style often seems to be a crapshoot.

In this chapter, we will suggest how your knowledge of personality types can bring a little reason and order to this process. We will first discuss how the personality type of our reader can tell us how formal or informal our writing should be. Then we will discuss four types of audiences: ST, SF, NT, and NF. These patterns are the same ones we have highlighted in previous chapters: combinations of our preference for either Sensing (S) or Intuition (N) with our preference for either Thinking (T) or Feeling (F). When reading this chapter, remember that it is always best to write your rough drafts in your own way, in the process and style that is best suited to your personality type. Once you have a rough draft, you then will be in a better position to think about how you should revise your style to suit the tastes of your audience.

Formality (IT) and Informality (EF)

In certain situations, it is more appropriate to be informal; in others, formality is the key. When we write for teachers or bosses, we generally try to be a little more formal than when we are writing for a good friend. Social situations certainly pressure us to act in specific ways, and certain types of people tend to naturally resort to either a formal or informal style.

Introverted Thinking types (IT), who naturally assume a formal stance toward people, generally write in a more formal style. Extraverted Feeling types (EF), who are naturally more casual and conversational, generally write in a more informal style. If, instead of these combinations, you are an IF or an ET type, your writing will generally have a mix of formal and informal qualities.

Why is all of this important? Imagine that you are an EF who typically writes in a rather conversational style. You have to write a memorandum for your IT boss. As an EF, you might produce a memorandum like this:

TO: Cyndy Freeman
FR: Bill Bateson
RE: Our widget problem

I know that you are wondering what is happening with our production of widgets! Well, we have run into a few BIG problems! I am quite distressed about this! And I know that you will be distressed also! So, I thought that I would write to you and give you the lowdown and I wanted to do that BEFORE you left for vacation! You see, the problem has to do with the cost of importing an important part from Korea, which has really slowed us down. Then, we became delayed with our schedule. What shall we do???

We do not want to suggest that all EFs would write a memorandum like this. But they are more likely to employ some of these conversational and informal features in their texts. Because this sample memorandum is intentionally meant to be an exaggeration, you would not be likely to find many people working in business who will so poorly understand the formality of the writing situation.

Nonetheless, the writing of EFs often reflects their tone of voice (exclamation points, multiple question marks, capital letters, underlining), conversational interjections ("well," "so," "then"), slang expressions ("the lowdown"), first and second person pronouns ("I" and "you"), and intensifiers ("very" and "really"). EFs are also more likely to include dialogue or a sense of dialogue (asking themselves questions and then answering them) and expressions of their feelings ("I am quite distressed about this!"). These features make for a less formal memorandum.

If we revise this memorandum by editing out some of these conversational features, it will be more appropriate for a business setting and a formal boss:

TO: Cynthia D. Freeman
     Production Manager
FR: William R. Bateson
     Assistant Production Manager
RE: Production schedule of widgets

I know that you are wondering what is happening with our production of widgets. We have run into a few problems.

The main problem has to do with the increased cost of an important part that we are importing from Korea, which has delayed our schedule.

I thought that I would write you about this matter before you left for vacation. Could you advise us on how to proceed?

This revision still has a general tone of informality, which is natural for an EF writer. But it is more mindful than the earlier example of the IT reader's need to get to the point more quickly. What we want to suggest with this example is that when writing in certain situations or for certain types of people, EFs need to make their writing a little more formal. Although formalizing one's writing might, at times, mean extensive rewriting, sometimes some simple editorial changes, as demonstrated above, will suffice.

We should also add that sometimes ITs may write too stiffly and formally. They can often loosen up their writing by "speaking" it. By this, we mean that they can produce a more informal style by speaking their letters or reports into a tape recorder or dictating machine and making a special effort to think of themselves as talking to a close friend instead of writing to a nameless or faceless reader. They can also add, in moderation, some of the oral features that come more naturally to EFs. Adding a few "well's" and "so's," for example, can do much to make stiff prose more friendly.

Writing for ST Audiences

Sensing Thinking (ST) types prefer writing that is factual, objective, clear, realistic, unambiguous, logical, and to the point. They want to know exactly what the problem is and how it can be fixed.

STs begin with a fact or statistic, provide a clear list of important items, and outline a series of steps to follow.

If we were to revise the widget memorandum for an ST reader, it might look like this:

TO: Cynthia D. Freeman
    Production Manager
FR: William R. Bateson
    Assistant Production Manager
RE: Production schedule of widgets

The production schedule of widgets has been delayed due to cost overruns.

We originally negotiated with Nikko, a Japanese firm, to make part #143.65 for $1.23 each. The production cost for this part has now risen to $1.78.

I suggest the following course of action:

1. Order only enough parts from Nikko to fulfill our current contract.
2. Begin immediate negotiations with other manufacturers.
3. Limit advertising and promotion of widgets.

This memorandum would appeal to most STs. First, it is clear, concise, and to the point. The problem is stated in the first sentence. Second, it is concrete and detailed. The name (or number) of the exact part in question is mentioned as well as the original and current cost. Third, a solution is presented, clearly broken down into a series of steps that need to be followed.

To some, this might seem like the perfect business memorandum. It follows the basic principles of business and technical writing, and there is a reason for this. STs are found in high numbers in technical fields and business administration, so it makes sense that this type of writing has come to be accepted as the norm. We should remember, however, that this type of writing is not suited for all situations nor for all audiences in engineering and business.

Writing for SF Audiences

Sensing Feeling types (SFs), while as appreciative of specifics, details, and clarity as STs, are more interested in writing that is about and addressed to specific people. They often find the writing of STs to be too dry and depersonalized. SF readers will respond best when a writer acknowledges them and others as individuals.

If we were to revise the widget memorandum for SFs, it might look like this:

TO: Cynthia D. Freeman
FR: William R. Bateson
RE: Production Schedule of Widgets

The production schedule of widgets has unfortunately been delayed due to cost overruns.

We originally negotiated with Tamiko Yakomoto of Nikko, a Japanese firm, to make part #143.65 for $1.23 each. The production cost for this part has now risen to $1.78.

When we questioned Mr. Yakomoto about the price increase, he apologized, saying that it was beyond his control.

He said that they imported some materials from Russia, and, due to changes in currency exchange, they have had to pay more for raw materials.

I suggest the following course of action for your approval:

1. Order only enough parts from Nikko to fulfill our current contract.
2. Begin immediate negotiations with other manufacturers.
3. Limit advertising and promotion of widgets.

Given my conversation with Mr. Yakomoto, I feel that he will understand our need to take this course of action.

I imagine that you are as disappointed about this problem as I am, but I do not feel that it will severely delay our production schedule.

I will wait for your advice and reactions before I initiate any actions.

In the first line of the memorandum, we added the word "unfortunately." Although this might appear to be a simple change, it makes the memorandum seem less sterile and devoid of emotions to SFs (and NFs as well). The references to Mr. Yakomoto and the empathic statement in the next to the last paragraph (an attempt to connect the writer's emotions with those of the reader) also help to further personalize the memorandum.

We do not typically think of business writing as a genre that allows us to be familiar and personal. However, a few simple changes such as those above can personalize a piece of writing without violating any sense of what is considered appropriate and acceptable.

Writing for NT Audiences

Intuitive Thinking types (NTs) prefer writing that goes beyond the mere facts of the situation. They also want a theoretical explanation. Their own writing, especially that of NTs in academic life, is usually rather abstract and philosophical. In the world of business, NTs learn to be more practical and to deal with important facts. But even in that context, they want to know the "why" behind the facts, and when they are dealing with a problem, they want to know how the system that created the problem can be changed so that it will not happen again.

Like the STs, NTs prefer writing that tends to be emotionally neutral. While the STs just want the facts, the NTs just want the interpretation.

If we were to revise the widget memorandum for an NT audience, it might look like this:

TO: Cynthia D. Freeman
       Production Manager
FR: William R. Bateson
       Assistant Production Manager
RE: Production schedule of widgets

The production schedule of widgets has been delayed due to cost overruns.

We originally negotiated with Nikko, a Japanese firm, to make part #143.65 for $1.23 each. The production cost for this part has now risen to $1.78.

I suggest the following course of action:

1. Order only enough parts from Nikko to fulfill our current contract. This will minimize any delays in the production of our widgets and will avoid problems with our distributors.

2. Begin immediate negotiations with other manufacturers. We will attempt to find another company that can produce part #143.65 at a lower cost and that can supply us with parts soon enough to avoid additional delays in our production schedule.

3. Limit advertising and promotion of widgets. Until we can secure part #143.65 at a lower cost, we should minimalize distribution and sales of widgets.

This memorandum answers some of the questions that NTs will naturally raise. It now states that this is not a systemic problem, but one that needs to be dealt with in isolation, and it provides explanations for each course of action.

Writing for NF Audiences

Intuitive Feeling types (NFs) prefer writing that builds a communication bridge between and among human beings. Their value for personalization is similar to that of SFs. But NFs are more likely to see people issues as part of a big picture rather than as relating to specific people. In their writing, they seek to foster a general spirit of human growth and goodwill.

If an NF were to read the ST widget memorandum, some questions might arise: How long has our company had a relationship with Nikko, the Japanese firm? Has this been a good, mutually beneficial relationship? How will our failure to renew our contract with Nikko affect this relationship? How will it affect the image of our company in the greater business community? Usually a writer will come across better to NFs when they show that they, too, have considered the people and relationship issues.

If the widget memorandum were revised for NFs, it might look like this:

TO: Cynthia D. Freeman
FR: William R. Bateson
RE: Production Schedule of Widgets

The production schedule of widgets has unfortunately been delayed due to cost overruns.

We originally negotiated with Nikko, a Japanese firm, to make part #143.65 for $1.23 each. The production cost for this part has now risen to $1.78.

This is the first contract that we have negotiated with Nikko. I suggest the following course of action:

1. Order only enough parts from Nikko to fulfill our current contract. This will minimize any delays in the production

of our widgets and will aviod problems with our distributors. By notifying Nikko that we will not be renewing our
contract, we will make every attempt to maintain a cordial
working relationship.

2. Begin immediate negotiations with other manufacturers.
   We will attempt to find another company that can produce
   part #143.65 at a lower cost and that can supply us with
   parts soon enough to avoid additional delays in our
   production schedule. We have several long-standing relations with other companies that might be able to produce the
   part at a lower cost than Nikko.

3. Limit advertising and promotion of widgets. Until we can
   secure part #143.65 at a lower cost, we should minimalize
   distribution and sales of widgets. We do not wish to create
   ill will by failing to meet demand or prematurely raising
   prices.

The concern for the personal and business relationships are certainly important for NF readers. But, even when not writing for NFs,
such comments can make for more meaningful and persuasive writing. Any issue, whether in politics, business, or some other field, goes
beyond the mere facts.

The contrasting danger, of course, is that an NF writer might tend
to overlook the necessary facts out of their greater concern for human
harmony. They might benefit from reading the ST example and drafting an occasional memorandum in a short, to-the-point fashion.

Thinking About Your Audience

How can what you have learned in this chapter help you as a writer?
When you are writing for a specific teacher, boss, or business associ-
ate, it is useful to think about what that person's type might be and
then adapt your writing to his or her preferred style. Different words
appeal to different personalities. Some of these words are shown on
the table on the following page. If you learn to speak the "language"
of your audience, your message is more likely to be heard.

Words That Appeal to Different Types

Extraverts (E)	Introverts (I)
experience	thoughtful
vitality	serious
lively	sincere
active	considered
doing	reflective
initiative	

Sensing Types (S)	Intuitive Types (N)
practical	innovative
realistic	possibilities
solid	hunches
concrete	inspiration
sensible	dream
here and now	imagination
responsible	depth
careful	

Thinking Types (T)	Feeling Types (F)
objectives	beliefs
analytical	values
logical	personal
valid	heartfelt
systematic	touching
evidence	invested
	we, us, together

Judging Types (J)	Perceiving Types (P)
complete	extensive
settled	in progress
finished	ongoing
hardworking	adaptable
punctual	flexible
decisive	open-minded
	questioning

When you are writing for broader audiences or entire groups of people, you may want to write a draft in your preferred style first and then revise it for the different types, adding a personal comment for the SFs, conceptual interpretation for the NTs, and so on. Then your message will be more likely to get across to a more diverse group of people.

Indeed, it is probably a good idea to generally revise all of your writing for different types of people. This will usually lead to a more well-considered piece of writing. Whenever one writes within an institution, whether it be a government agency or a corporation, one should remember that writing lives on in people's files. A memorandum that you may have intended one person to read and discard can be picked up years later by someone else. So it makes sense to generally write the kind of texts that will be suited, at least somewhat, for broader audiences.

Finally, you may want to use type theory to help you analyze the flow of communication within your organization. A few years ago, we were consulting with a large mortgage firm. The executive over a division of underwriters had complaints from mortgage brokers that letters coming from the underwriters were too harsh and cold. We made some initial assumptions about the personality type of the key figures in the chain of command, but we found a perplexing bottleneck. To our surprise, many of the underwriters were NFs and were writing very personal and unthreatening letters to brokers, the kind of letters that the executive in charge of the division (who we predicted was an INFJ) wanted to see. But all of the letters had to be approved (and revised) by a middle manager, who appeared to be an ESTJ. The problem with the letters was not that the underwriters needed to improve their writing skills (as was first assumed), but that the ESTJ middle manager required the underwriters to revise their letters until they sounded "businesslike"—objective, distant, to the point, and often harsh. Once the ESTJ let the original letters go through, the executive, as well as the brokers, were pleased with the style of the letters.

Whenever you are writing in a business setting, you have to remember that you do not have a single audience. Rather, you have levels of audiences. You have to write for the person who will eventually read your letters, memoranda, or reports, but you also have to write for middle managers, managers, and executives who have to approve your prose before it is sent on. It is useful, therefore, to make a flowchart of your company, listing all of the people who have to approve your drafts and what you think that their personality type is. Then you will be much better equipped to think about the complex process of writing within a corporation or bureaucracy.

Collaboration:
Writing With
Friends and Enemies

Susan and Maria, both composition teachers at a major university, had offices across the hall from each other. When they collaborated on writing projects, each would sit at her desk in her own office, but with the doors open, to actually write together—and we mean together. They talked out a text that Maria punched into her word processor. Susan might talk out the first few sentences of a paragraph, and then Maria would finish it. Or, Maria might begin talking about a vague thought and Susan would rephrase it until, between them, they had produced a clear, fully developed idea that could be added to their emerging text.

For some people, this is how the creative process works best. A group of people sit around together and talk out their ideas. In the beginning, most of the ideas are fairly hairbrained, but sooner or later something happens. It seems like the energy of hearing each other talk about bad ideas eventually generates some good ones.

This group approach to brainstorming and writing works quite well for most Extraverts. They need to hear their own ideas and sense how these ideas affect others to do their best work. When they are forced to work in isolation, Extraverts may feel sluggish and have trouble getting a handle on their thoughts.

But this approach probably sounds like pure hell for the average Introvert. We are both Introverts, and we could not conceive of collaborating as Susan and Maria do. We prefer to come together to discuss the project in broad terms. Then we divide the work up and go off to our own offices, far away from each other, to write. When we finish a decent draft, we pass it on and let our coauthor revise it. Draft after draft is exchanged, perhaps with some comments over the phone or in person about what was changed and why, but the revising—as with the initial composing—is always done in private. We collaborate by seemingly working alone.

But I never collaborate when I write, you may be thinking. I just have to work independently. At a concrete level, perhaps you are right.

Yet whenever a teacher, colleague, or boss returns your draft to you with comments or suggestions on it, your revising process becomes collaborative. When the members of your staff at work or your thesis committee in graduate school each have different standards, your wish for autonomy in writing is compromised. An editor or a proofreader can sometimes enter our imagination even as we sit alone generating ideas for our next piece.

Whether our collaborations are deliberate (as with coauthors) or implied (as with readers' responses, actual or imagined), it is tricky to maintain a sense of our own voice or natural style while at the same time achieving a sensitivity to the insights or methods that others bring to the project. In music, two or more soloists can perform successfully together, each with his or her unique expressiveness. But the performers also need to listen as well as project and to blend their sounds with those of their partners, both harmoniously and musically. Collaboration in writing is much the same.

It might seem, at this point, as if collaboration always works better when the coauthors are the same personality type. Although it might be true that such collaborations work more smoothly, not much is gained by sharing similar perspectives. As in marriage, collaboration benefits from the union of differing talents. When we are forced to acknowledge a different perspective, that of our spouse or coauthor, we can make better decisions, recognize our own shortcomings, draw from the other person's strengths, and experience a wonderful opportunity to grow and mature.

In this chapter, we will discuss some of the difficulties and benefits of writing with others of similar or dissimilar type. We hope that it will make your collaborations less stressful and more productive and, as a result, help you write with friends rather than enemies. The charts on the following pages suggest a number of strategies for making contact with different types of collaborators and list some specific areas in which different types may experience a breakdown in communication.

Extraversion and Introversion

As illustrated by the examples above, Extraverts who write with Extraverts are more likely to compose and revise together, working in close proximity and talking out a text. Marianne Walters and three other noted family therapists collaborated in the writing of *The Invisible Web: Gender Patterns in Family Relationships*. Her description of their work together reflects the value that Extraverts place on lively interaction in writing projects.

> Our collaboration became one of the few arenas where we could be endlessly contradicted and challenged. From the beginning, the Women's Project had been a place where we vigorously debated our ideas.... The process of reading our work aloud to each other and opening ourselves up to criticism, challenge, and disagreement put us in a context of intense proximity requiring both trust and respect for our individual differences.

Extraverts seem to gain a great deal of energy from their rapid exchange of ideas. The most serious danger that they may encounter is that they might "hyper each other into a frenzy." By this, a line borrowed from the movie *The Big Chill*, we mean that they might generate so much energy and have so many ideas flying around the room that they are unable to bring a focus to their text. Extraverts often think of so many ideas so quickly that they are unable to develop them or pull them together. They might even develop ideas so quickly that they become bored with the entire process.

This kind of interactive, high-energy group-writing process is often used in business, especially by people in the creative side of advertising. We have all seen such scenes in movies or television shows.

Strategies for Making Contact With Collaborators

Extraversion (E)	Introversion (I)
The best way to make contact with Extraverts is through their preferred channel of communication: talk. They usually respond better to oral than to written feedback. Since they value active experience, they respond well to compliments about the vitality and energy of their writing.	Introverts respond better to any situation when given advance notice and when not expected to "think on their feet." It is best to first provide them with an agenda, and follow up later. This will allow them to think about what they may want to say. Introverts often respond well to teachers who acknowledge that they have more to say (or write) than they have offered. They will talk (or write) more when they trust their teacher and when they are not forced to share their ideas.

Sensing (S)	Intuition (N)
Sensing types attend better to communications that begin with the concrete. Facts, concrete examples, and practical solutions appeal to them. They respond well to compliments about being accurate, reliable, and precise.	Intuitive types attend better to communications that begin with concepts, theories, or inferences. They like sentences that begin with "What if...." They value being innovative, original, and theoretical.

From *Personality and the Teaching of Composition* by George H. Jensen and John K. DiTiberio, pp. 113–114. Norwood, NJ: Ablex, 1989. Copyright 1989 by Ablex. Reprinted by permission from Ablex Publishing Corporation.

Strategies for Making Contact With Collaborators (continued)

Thinking (T)	Feeling (F)
Thinking types value being logical and objective. They react most favorably to a rationale and logical, analytical thought. They prefer criticism that is to the point rather than criticism that is softened or indirect. Praise should, at least in part, relate to the content of their writing.	Feeling types tend to respond well to communication after personal contact has been made. They prefer to chat informally before getting down to business, especially if they are also Extraverts. They respond well to any acknowledgment of themselves as individuals: learning their name, asking about their interests and values, a pat on the back, and so forth. They often respond well to an instructor saying that he or she enjoyed reading their essays. Praise should, at least in part, relate to the process of their writing, for example, the way they worded their ideas.

Judging (J)	Perceiving (P)
Judging types are particularly concerned about wise use of time and usually respond well to compliments about how efficient, expedient, or punctual they are. They also value being decisive. They tend to view their work, once it is submitted, as finished, and prefer to hear comments about how they can improve the next essay rather than this one.	Perceiving types are usually most concerned about being inclusive, so they tend to respond well to compliments about the breadth of their research. They tend to view their work as ongoing. They prefer to hear about how to improve this essay rather than about how to improve the next essay. They also like to see how one project can relate to the next, even though they are both unfinished.

Four or five people sit in a room talking out loud, finishing each other's sentences. But not everyone will like this process. Introverts will often find themselves becoming extremely fatigued after a brief exposure to a session of group writing or brainstorming. They would much rather sit alone at their desk, stare out the window, and think of a list of ideas that could later be shared with the rest of their creative group. When Extraverted bosses want to employ this kind of group writing session, they should give the topic to everyone in advance. This will allow the Introverts to prepare for the talk session by thinking about the topic and making some notes. When these sessions begin to lose steam or stall, bosses are advised to switch to a more Introverted approach for a little while. This will allow the Introverts—in their more natural mode of working—to reflect on the problem and seek a solution that can move the process on to the next stage. Such breaks can also help the Extraverts, who might have been pursuing an unproductive line of thought. With some time off, they can resume their talks from a fresh starting point.

It is also important to understand how Extraverts and Introverts view each other in this kind of group process. Introverts might be continually thrown off balance by the Extravert's rapid exploration of ideas. Because Extraverts quickly throw out ideas, often with little or no reflection, their thoughts might seem contradictory or scattered to an Introvert. Introverts need to realize that Extraverts are not committed to every idea that they voice. As a general rule, if you do not like what an Extravert is saying, wait a few minutes. Another idea, perhaps even the opposite idea, will soon be voiced. Introverts can help Extraverts bring a focus to their ideas by listening and reacting—preferably with some excitement—to what they consider to be good ideas.

When writing as a group, Extraverts may view Introverts as disconnected, not doing their part. But they need to realize that Introverts, even though they may throw out fewer ideas, will often be the ones to save a good idea from a rapid exchange of bad ideas. Introverts can thus bring a focus and coherence to the process. Indeed, when the group seems to be spinning its wheels, it is beneficial to stop and ask the Introverts to recall some of the good ideas that they feel were passed over too quickly.

Breakdowns in Collaboration

Extraversion (E)	Introversion (I)
Extraverts may become annoyed at the reticence of Introverts, feeling a social obligation to keep the conversation going. They may fail to recognize the thought and seriousness that goes into an Introvert's seemingly off-the-cuff statement.	When Extraverts press an Introvert to become more talkative, the Introvert may withdraw from social interaction. Introverts may assume that Extraverts have made up their minds when they are just brainstorming out loud.

Sensing (S)	Intuition (N)
A Sensing type may become lost amid an Intuitive type's quickness to move to abstractions. They may feel the work of Intuitives is not practical.	Intuitive types may become overwhelmed by the sheer volume of facts presented by Sensing types. They may become frustrated when the Sensing type tells them something will not work.

Thinking (T)	Feeling (F)
Thinking types may see an emotional issue in logical terms; rather than attempting to understand how the Feeling type feels, they may try to explain why he or she is thinking illogically. Thinking types may be overly blunt. They usually want to attend to business before socializing.	Feeling types may mistake the Thinking type's intensity about ideas for anger; rather than join in the excitement, they may feel hurt and withdraw. They may withhold comments or soften them to the point that they are not very clear. They usually want to socialize first, establish or reestablish the relationship, then attend to business.

Judging (J)	Perceiving (P)
Judging types may become annoyed at the slowness of Perceiving types to reach decisions or to stick with those decisions once made.	Perceiving types may feel overly pressured by Judging types to reach closure and finish projects.

When Extraverts collaborate with a single Introvert, they need to realize that their preferred intense interaction with another writer while in the act of composition will place the Introvert at a disadvantage. As with the group project, they need to allow their partner to have periodic escapes from the Extraverted activity so that he or she can rest and reflect on the process. Otherwise, the collaboration will rarely work, and the Introvert will feel overwhelmed.

Furthermore, the silence of an Introvert should not be misconstrued by Extraverts as a lack of involvement in the collaboration. Introverts do their best thinking away from the team, just as Extraverts do their best thinking when speaking with others.

Introverts who write with other Introverts are more likely to interact for brief periods—just long enough to make sure that they are both moving in the same general direction—and then move into seclusion to compose and revise. They are more likely to appoint one of the team to draft the text or divide the text into parts, parceling out the responsibility for drafting different sections. They rarely actually write together. If they are bosses, Introverts are more likely to assign one person the responsibility of drafting the text and then allow others to rewrite it.

Although the Introverted process can be efficient, not consuming the time of the entire group, the inherent problem with it is that the writers working in isolation might not be on the same wavelength. They might develop different expectations of what the end product should look like, or draft pieces of a text that are so different that they cannot be patched together.

Certainly, when the Introverted process is employed, everyone involved needs to strive to share their individual visions and clarify expectations. It is also important to share initial drafts—rather than completed products—so that any misperception of the project or miscommunication of expectations can be cleared up early in the writing process.

When Extraverts enter the Introvert's world to colloborate, they are likely to feel shut out, frustrated, and even intimidated by the Introvert's desire to find some space. One solution that we have seen work is for the Extravert to talk out a rough draft to the Introvert; the Introvert, in isolation, can prepare a draft of what the Extravert said—shaping, expanding, and reworking the Extravert's words as needed. Then the two can come back together to make final revisions.

Sensing and Intuition

When people of similar types collaborate, they tend to work more efficiently, but the characteristics of their preferences tend to become more exaggerated. For example, when two or more Sensing types collaborate, their writing tends to be even more filled with facts and details and more lacking in ideas and theory. When two Intuitive types collaborate, their writing tends to be especially filled with ideas and theory and lacking in facts and details. Collaboration with other people of a similar type, then, tends to make us think and act even more purely within our preferences than we would if writing alone. As a homogeneous group, we are less well balanced than as individuals.

This is why collaboration can be so valuable. We can work with someone of an opposite type and draw from his or her strengths. Sensing types can restrain Intuitive coauthors from becoming too scattered, and Intuitive types can help Sensing coauthors see the possibilities and understand the implications of their data.

This is not to say that Sensing and Intuitive types will never clash. When they do, they will generally argue over the unstated assumptions behind their procedures and methodology. Sensing types are more likely to use standard procedures—the solution or method that has proved successful in the past—while Intuitive types are more likely to develop their own procedures, ones that evolve from their theories and ideas. Intuitive types often struggle to convince a Sensing type to try a new method, and they may have difficulty understanding why a Sensing type is sticking with a tried-and-true procedure just because it worked in the past.

Because this clash is often one that involves unstated assumptions, it can be a hard one to get out into the open and resolve unless Sensing and Intuitive types make an effort to explain what they are doing.

Thinking and Feeling

Thinking and Feeling types communicate from opposing directions. Thinking types tend to concentrate on the content of what they are trying to say; they believe that it is best to say something directly and clearly. They believe that if they state their message clearly, their audience will listen. Feeling types are far more concerned with how the message is connecting with their audience. They want to capture their audience's attention, entertain them (especially if also Extraverted), and, most of all, avoid insulting them. Sometimes, their message may not be all that clear. It will be worded tentatively, hedged so that they do not say something that might separate them from their audience.

Both types can certainly learn from each other, but they need to appreciate the differences in their approaches to writing, even down to the very type of words that they choose. Thinking types tend to prefer technical words, the jargon that makes up the specialized language of a field. Feeling types tend to prefer words that are more personal or more poetic. Thinking types will often be surprised at how much time Feeling types will devote to revising single words. They will shift back and forth among five or six possible words or phrases when, to a Thinking type, the sentence is already clear and needs no further work. Feeling types will often find that their Thinking type collaborators use a language that is too dry and boring and distances the writer from the reader.

While these territorial battles over the right word might sometimes disrupt the collaboration of Thinking and Feeling types, what is more likely to cause serious rifts is how they give each other feedback. Thinking types will be a little more likely to discuss what is wrong and what needs to be changed, leaving compliments and praise unspoken. The Feeling type, who wants to connect with his or her coauthor as much as with the audience, may feel constantly off balance by the Thinking type's lack of praise. The Feeling type will wonder, Does my coauthor hate what I wrote? Is it really okay? What does my coauthor really think of me as a writer? One of the Thinking type's favorite words of praise—"interesting"—may send Feeling types reeling. Rather than interpret it as it was meant, as a compliment, and a simple statement that their partner has produced an interesting idea, Feeling types may assume that the Thinking type is using a vague word to avoid saying something negative.

Feeling types are a little more likely to deliver praise to their coauthors, sometimes to the point of not talking about needed changes to avoid the possibility of hurting the coauthor's feelings. What might surprise many Feeling types is that Thinking types often find excessive praise annoying. They generally prefer praise that is delivered more directly and with as little emotion as possible. Thinking types might say to themselves, Why won't my coauthor just cut the bull and get to the point? This is not to say that Thinking types don't need praise or don't need to know what they have done well. They just prefer the praise to be stated directly, more like this: "This is a great chapter. I have a few suggestions for you. I think that your introduction needs to do more to capture the reader's attention...."

Feeling types can also overwhelm their coauthors with the amount of feedback that they give. In general, Feeling types will write more comments on a coauthor's work than Thinking types. If the coauthor is a Feeling type, she might assume that her draft is beyond hope. If the coauthor is a Thinking type, she might feel that her coauthor is being needlessly picky.

Judging and Perceiving

It is almost inevitable that Judging types, who want to push toward meeting deadlines at all costs, and Perceiving types, who are more concerned about doing things thoroughly, will clash as coauthors. In John Grisham's popular mystery novel *The Pelican Brief*, the culminating scene involves a collaborative writing of the headline article exposing members of the federal government on a number of charges. The law student who first discovered the fraud (Darby Shaw) and the journalist (Gray Grantham) approached the task very differently, reflecting the different approaches of Judging and Perceiving types:

> Darby was a model of organization, with notes neatly arranged on the table, and words carefully written on paper.

He [Gray] was a whirlwind of chaos—papers on the floor, talking to the computer, printing random paragraphs that were discarded by the time they were on paper.

We have certainly experienced this kind of frustration in our own collaborations. The way that we tend to handle it is that George, the Judging type, tends to do our first drafts. He then sends them off to John, the Perceiving type, for revisions. Sometimes John's revisions are so thorough that it is almost as if he had started from scratch.

While collaborating on another book, John decided to immerse himself in one last major revision just as we were about to submit the final manuscript, or so George thought. George felt frustrated that John was delaying the completion of the project, and John felt annoyed that George was not willing to wait another week or two to make the manuscript even better.

Whenever clashes like this occur, we have found that it is very useful to discuss them within the framework of type differences. It helps George to know that John's apparent lack of concern for deadlines is related to many of his strengths as a writer. He is a thorough reviser and editor, he helps George expand and qualify his ideas, and he keeps George from submitting manuscripts that are not really finished. It similarly helps John know that George's single-minded push to meet deadlines is associated with strengths. George helps John push projects through to completion, avoid overqualifying good ideas until they lose all force of conviction, and know when revisions of revisions actually begin to make the text worse.

Conclusion

Every collaboration between two or more writers, even when they are of the same type, will experience some tension. When collaborating, the important thing is to learn from each other, use the encounter of different personality types and ideologies to grow as writers and people, and find a way to get past the deadlocks and the disagreements in some productive way. We have found that type theory can help with this process. If nothing else, it helps us to understand that the behavior that creates tension comes from the same psychological process —the same type preference—that produces other behaviors that we value. It gives us the big picture and encourages a little tolerance.

Epilogue:
Types, Stereotypes,
and Book Reports

A reader who quickly glances through this book might stop at certain pages and conclude that in describing types of writers, we come dangerously close to treating them as stereotypes. We believe the distinction between *type* and *stereotype* to be an important one. This concluding section is intended to illustrate the difference.

We all remember having to write book reports in elementary school. As young writers, our reactions to the assignment may have varied according to our own abilities as writers and the particular book we had to review, but our personality type also played a role in the kind of report that we produced.

In a scene from the musical play *You're a Good Man, Charlie Brown* called "The Book Report," four characters, each a distinct personality type, sing and talk about their school assignment. To illustrate each type's experience of the book report, we have chosen here to separate out the script for each character, even though on stage, the interaction is much more fluid.

Lucy's approach is both concrete and disdainful, reflecting a reponse to writing common to ST types when they are not clear about the rationale for the assignment:

> *Peter Rabbit* is this stupid book about this stupid rabbit who steals vegetables from other people's gardens (She counts the words, one through seventeen). Eighty-three to go.... The other people's name was MacGregor. (She counts the words from eighteen to twenty-three).... The name of the rabbit was Peter. Twenty-four, twenty-five.... There were

vegetables in the garden...such as carrots and spinach and onions and...lettuce and turnips and parsley and okra and cabbage and string beans and parsnips, tomatoes, potatoes.... *Peter Rabbit* is this stupid book about a stupid rabbit who steals vegetables from other people's gardens. Gardens, gardens. Seventy-five, seventy-six.... And they were very, very, very, very, very, very happy to be home.... Ninety-four, ninety-five. The very, very, very end.

Schroeder's approach, in contrast, is more enthusiastic, albeit rather scattered, like that of young NF types:

A book report on *Peter Rabbit.* The name of the book about which this book report is about is *Peter Rabbit,* which is about this rabbit. I found it very—(He crosses out). I liked the part where—(He crosses out). It was a —(Slash!). It reminded me of Robin Hood. And the part where Little John jumped from the rock to the Sheriff of Nottingham's back. And then Robin and everyone swung from the trees in a sudden surprise attack. And they captured the Sheriff and all of his goods, and they carried him back to their camp in the woods, and the Sheriff was guest at their dinner and all, but he wriggled away and he sounded the call, and his men rushed in and the arrows flew—Peter Rabbit did sort of that kind of thing too.... Down came the staff on his head—smash! And Robin fell like a sack full of lead—crash! The Sheriff laughed and he left him for dead—ha! But he was wrong.... Just then an arrow flew in—whing! It was the sign for the fight to begin—zing! And then it looked like the Sheriff would win—ah! But not for long. Away they ran. Just like rabbits, who run a lot, as you can tell from the story of Peter Rabbit, which this report is about.... The name of the book about which this book report is about is *Peter Rabbit, Peter Rabbit.* All for one, every man does his part. Oh—The end.

Linus' approach appears the most confident, and represents the dispassionate, categorical, academic style of NT types:

> A book report on *Peter Rabbit*. In examining a work such as *Peter Rabbit*, it is important that the superficial characteristics of its deceptively simple plot should not be allowed to blind the reader to the more substantial fabric of its deeper motivations. In this report I plan to discuss the sociological implications of family pressures so great as to drive an otherwise moral rabbit to perform acts of thievery which he consciously knew were against the law. I also hope to explore the personality of Mr. MacGregor in his conflicting roles as farmer and humanitarian.... Peter Rabbit is established from the start as a benevolent hero and it is only with the increase of social pressure that the seams in his moral fabric.... Not to mention the extreme pressure exerted on him by his deeply rooted rivalry with Flopsy, Mopsy, and Cottontail.... A-men.

Charlie Brown's approach shows him to be most traumatized by the assignment. Like SF types, he wants to please, but he feels intimidated and torn between the "shoulds" of writing on the one hand and those of being "outside playing":

> A book report on *Peter Rabbit*.... If I start writing now when I'm not really rested it could upset my thinking which is not good at all. I'll get a fresh start tomorrow and it's not due till Wednesday, so I'll have all of Tuesday unless something should happen. Why does this always happen—I should be outside playing, getting fresh air and sunshine, I work best under pressure and there'll be lots of pressure if I wait till tomorrow, I should start writing now. But if I start writing now when I'm not really rested, it could upset my thinking which is not good at all.... How do they expect us to write a book report...of any quality in just two days.... How can they conspire to make life so miserable, and so effectively

in so many ways.... If I start writing now when I'm not really rested it could upset my thinking which is not good at all. No good at all. Oh—first thing after dinner I'll start.

Charlie Brown's final soliloquy in this section reflects the typical source of refuge and strength for SF types under stress—he notices a little leaf, its "courage and tenacity" and "the strength of his convictions":

> You know, I don't know if you'll understand this or not, but sometimes, even when I'm feeling very low, I'll see some little thing that will somehow renew my faith. Just something like that leaf, for instance—clinging to its tree in spite of wind and storm. You know, that makes me think that courage and tenacity are about the greatest values that a man can have. Suddenly my old confidence is back and I know things aren't half as bad as I make them out to be. Suddenly I know that with the strength of his convictions a man can move mountains, and I can proceed with full confidence in the basic goodness of my fellow man. I know that now. I know it.

Because characters on a stage tend to have a rather pure form, we can treat Charlie Brown and his classmates as types with a degree of confidence. Playwrights, novelists, and other creative artists for generations have contrasted their characters in this way to help us see the dynamic tension among them.

It is similarly tempting to read a section of a written text and conclude that we know definitively the personality type of the author. We cannot. To hypothesize about the personality of writers can certainly help us learn about and understand variations in the ways people go about such tasks. Any attempt to foster an appreciation for diversity is worthwhile, we believe. But there is a fine line between gaining a perspective on differences on the one hand and reducing people to fixed categories on the other. The former is the appropriate endeavor of Jung's type theory. The latter involves stereotypes.

As used in this book, the concept of *type* is one that recognizes fundamental predispositions and natural preferences, perhaps inborn.

But biology is not destiny. To prefer outward activity and learning by trial and error (Extraversion) does not limit us only to those activities. Many Extraverts, for example, appear quiet, reserved, and very inward in their focus, depending in part on the demands of the situation, their level of functioning (either that day or in general), cultural or family influences and models, and their personal needs at this point in their development. Stereotypes, by definition, are static, rigid, and usually demeaning. Types, as defined by Jung and Briggs and Myers and as presented in this book, are general patterns toward which people lean, each with its own virtues. The most successful writers discover their preferred patterns, find ways to operationalize them, and then employ contrasting methods or aspects of their personality as the situation demands and as they mature.

Just as importantly, the style and substance of people's writing changes as they learn new skills and ways to craft their texts. Writing bears the stamp not only of one's personal signature, but of the influence of teachers, professions, and the broader society and era in which one lives. When we quoted in earlier chapters from the writing of certain types, we selected pieces that fit the general pattern for illustration. As we attempted to make clear, those very writers often produced vastly different texts at different times while we worked with them. We must always distinguish one's natural predisposition from one's ability to perform behaviors.

It is fun, and also instructive, to make educated guesses about the personality behind the writing of Ernest Hemingway or Maya Angelou, of Annie Dillard or Mark Twain, of Abraham Lincoln or Winston Churchill. That is why we included excerpts from the writings or autobiographies of these and other noted authors.

Students, teachers, and schools have lately come under attack for not giving sufficient attention to the basic tools required of a "literate" American. Some have suggested a single solution to the problem—a common fund of knowledge and skills required for all citizens. Such arguments reduce all writers and readers to two kinds: those who are truly literate and those who are not. In our view, this represents stereotyping at its most insidious.

As we hope this book points out, there are multiple ways of developing ideas, of putting words to paper, or of interpreting texts when we read them. Truly "literate" Americans, we believe, come in all kinds. They might write vastly different reports of what they saw when they visited an innercity park in Atlanta, as did the four writers in chapter 8. They compose distinctly different perceptions of a "Spring Day," as did the two writers in chapter 6, or of a "Christmas Tree," as did the four writers in chapter 7. They will produce unique drafts of a book report, as did Charlie Brown and his friends. All of these products may be flawed; each may also possess the rudiments of a successful beginning draft that the others are lacking.

We believe the distinction between stereotypes and type patterns is a vital one. The one approach reduces people to caricatures; the other affirms people's preferences while encouraging development within their type.

We hope that your reading of this book has helped you to understand the natural strengths of your type of person and to find ways you might approach writing with more confidence and success.

Appendix

Characteristics Frequently Associated With Each Type

Sensing Types

Introverts	**ISTJ** Serious, quiet, earn success by concentration and thoroughness. Practical, orderly, matter-of-fact, logical, realistic, and dependable. See to it that everything is well organized. Take responsibility. Make up their own minds as to what should be accomplished and work toward it steadily, regardless of protests or distractions.	**ISFJ** Quiet, friendly, responsible, and conscientious. Work devotedly to meet their obligations. Lend stability to any project or group. Thorough, painstaking, and accurate. Their interests are usually not technical. Can be patient with necessary details. Loyal, considerate, perceptive, concerned with how other people feel.
	ISTP Cool onlookers—quiet, reserved, observing and analyzing life with detached curiosity and unexpected flashes of original humor. Usually interested in cause and effect, how and why mechanical things work, and organizing facts using logical principles. Excel at getting to the core of a practical problem and finding the solution.	**ISFP** Retiring, quietly friendly, sensitive, kind, modest about their abilities. Shun disagreements, do not force their opinions or values on others. Usually do not care to lead but are often loyal followers. Often relaxed about getting things done because they enjoy the present moment and do not want to spoil it by undue haste or exertion.
Extraverts	**ESTP** Good at on-the-spot problem solving. Like action, enjoy whatever comes along. Tend to like mechanical things and sports, with friends on the side. Adaptable, tolerant, pragmatic; focused on getting results. Dislike long explanations. Are best with real things that can be worked, handled, taken apart, or put together.	**ESFP** Outgoing, accepting, friendly, enjoy everything and make things more fun for others by their enjoyment. Like action and making things happen. Know what's going on and join in eagerly. Find remembering facts easier than mastering theories. Are best in situations that need sound common sense and practical ability with people.
	ESTJ Practical, realistic, matter-of-fact, with a natural head for business or mechanics. Not interested in abstract theories; want learning to have direct and immediate application. Like to organize and run activities. Often make good administrators; are decisive, quickly move to implement decisions; take care of routine details.	**ESFJ** Warm-hearted, talkative, popular, conscientious, born cooperators, active committee members. Need harmony and may be good at creating it. Always doing something nice for someone. Work best with encouragement and praise. Main interest is in things that directly and visibly affect people's lives.

Characteristics Frequently Associated With Each Type (con't)

Intuitive Types

INFJ	INTJ
Succeed by perseverance, originality, and desire to do whatever is needed or wanted. Put their best efforts into their work. Quietly forceful, conscientious, concerned for others. Respected for their firm principles. Likely to be honored and followed for their clear visions as to how best to serve the common good.	Have original minds and great drive for their own ideas and purposes. Have long-range vision and quickly find meaningful patterns in external events. In fields that appeal to them, they have a fine power to organize a job and carry it through. Skeptical, critical, independent, determined, have high standards of competence and performance.

INFP	INTP
Quiet observers, idealistic, loyal. Important that outer life be congruent with inner values. Curious, quick to see possibilities, often serve as catalysts to implement ideas. Adaptable, flexible, and accepting unless a value is threatened. Want to understand people and ways of fulfilling human potential. Little concern with possessions or surroundings.	Quiet and reserved. Especially enjoy theoretical or scientific pursuits. Like solving problems with logic and analysis. Interested mainly in ideas, with little liking for parties or small talk. Tend to have sharply defined interests. Need careers where some strong interest can be used and useful.

(right margin: Introverts)

ENFP	ENTP
Warmly enthusiastic, high-spirited, ingenious, imaginative. Able to do almost anything that interests them. Quick with a solution for any difficulty and ready to help anybody with a problem. Often rely on their ability to improvise instead of preparing in advance. Can usually find compelling reasons for whatever they want.	Quick, ingenious, good at many things. Stimulating company, alert and outspoken. May argue for fun on either side of a question. Resourceful in solving new and challenging problems, but may neglect routine assignments. Apt to turn to one new interest after another. Skillful in finding logical reasons for what they want.

ENFJ	ENTJ
Responsive and responsible. Feel real concern for what others think or want, and try to handle things with due regard for other's feelings. Can present a proposal or lead a group discussion with ease and tact. Sociable, popular, sympathetic. Responsive to praise and criticism. Like to facilitate others and enable people to achieve their potential.	Frank, decisive, leaders in activities. Develop and implement comprehensive systems to solve organizational problems. Good at anything that requires reasoning and intelligent talk, such as public speaking. Are usually well-informed and enjoy adding to their fund of knowledge.

(right margin: Extraverts)

Bibliography

Angelou, Maya. *I Know Why the Caged Bird Sings,* p. 77. New York: Bantam Books, 1969.

Associated Press. "Clinton Makes His Daily Journal a Tale of the Tape," *St. Louis Post-Dispatch,* November 2, 1993, p. 3A.

Caputo, Philip. "Styron's Choices," *Esquire,* December, 1986, p. 152.

Davis, J. Madison. *Conversations With Robertson Davies,* p. 83. Jackson: University Press of Mississippi, 1989.

Dillard, Annie. *The Writing Life,* pp. 26, 31, 68, 79. New York: Harper Perennial, 1989.

DiTiberio, John K. and Allen L. Hammer. *Introduction to Type in College.* Palo Alto, CA: Consulting Psychologists Press, 1993.

Doctorow, E. L. "Braver Than We Thought." Review of Ernest Hemingway's *The Garden of Eden, New York Times Book Review,* May 18, 1986, pp. 1, 44.

Elbow, Peter. *Writing With Power: Techniques for Mastering the Writing Process.* New York: Oxford, 1981.

Ephron, Nora. "Revision and Life: Take It From the Top—Again," *New York Times Book Review,* November 9, 1986, p. 7.

Gesner, Clark. *You're a Good Man, Charlie Brown,* pp. 36–44. New York: Random House, 1967.

Goldberg, Natalie. *Writing Down the Bones: Freeing the Writer Within,* p. 5. New York: Quality Paperback Book Club, 1986.

Grisham, John. *The Pelican Brief,* p. 393. New York: Dell, 1992.

Hampl, Patricia. "The Need to Say It." In *The Writer on Her Work.* Vol. 2, *New Essays in New Territory,* edited by Janet Sternberg, pp. 21–22. New York: Norton, 1991.

Hemingway, Ernest. *The Garden of Eden,* p. 37. New York: Collier Books, 1986.

Hirsch, E. D., Jr. *Cultural Literacy: What Every American Needs to Know,* pp. 27–28, 133. New York: Vintage Books, 1987.

Hirsh, Sandra and Jean Kummerow. *LifeTypes.* NewYork: Warner Books, 1989.

Isaacs, Susan. Review of James A. Michener's *The Novel. New York Times Book Review,* March 31, 1991, p. 12.

James, Caryn. "Auteur! Auteur!" p. 20. *New York Times Magazine*, January 19, 1986.

Jensen, George H. "Consulting with 'Discursive Regimes': Using Personality Theory to Analyze and Intervene in Business Communities." In *Worlds of Writing: Teaching and Learning in Discourse Communities of Work*, edited by Carolyn B. Matalene, pp. 291–301. New York: Random House, 1989.

Jensen, George H. *From Texts to Text: Mastering Academic Discourse*, pp. 468–473. New York: HarperCollins, 1991.

Jensen, George H. "Learning Styles." In *Applications of the Myers-Briggs Type Indicator in Higher Education*, edited by Judith Provost and Scott Anchors, pp. 181–208. Palo Alto, CA: Consulting Psychologists Press, 1987.

Jensen, George H. and John K. DiTiberio. "The MBTI and Writing Blocks," *MBTI News*, 5 (1983): pp. 14–15.

Jensen, George H. and John K. DiTiberio. "Personality and Individual Writing Processes." *College Composition and Communication*, 35 (1984): pp. 285–300.

Jensen, George H. and John K. DiTiberio. *Personality and the Teaching of Composition*, pp. ix, 98–99, 113–114. Norwood, NJ: Ablex, 1989.

Jung, Carl G. *Psychological Types*. New York: Harcourt Brace, 1923.

Keirsey, David and Marilyn Bates. *Please Understand Me: An Essay on Temperament Styles*. Del Mar, CA: Prometheus Nemesis, 1978.

Kohl, Herbert R. "The Open Classroom." *The New York Review of Books* (1969).

Kroeger, Otto and Janet Thuesen. *Type Talk: The Sixteen Personality Types that Determine How We Live, Love and Work*. New York: Delta, 1988.

Lawrence, Gordon. *People Types and Tiger Stripes*. Gainesville, FL: Center for Applications of Psychological Type, 1993.

Lawton, David. "Composition Courses for College Freshmen are Ineffective; They Should Be Abolished," *The Chronicle of Higher Education*, September 21, 1988, p. B1.

Lindemann, Erika. *A Rhetoric for Writing Teachers*. New York: Oxford, 1987.

Manchester, William. *Winston Spencer Churchill: The Last Lion*. Vol. 2. *Alone 1932–1940*, pp. 11, 33. Boston: Little, Brown, 1988.

Martin, Ralph G. *A Hero for Our Time: An Intimate Story of the Kennedy Years*, p. 140. New York: Fawcett Crest, 1983.

McPhee, John. "Writers and Their Works: A Question-Answer Session With John McPhee," Conference on College Composition and Communication, St. Louis, Missouri, March 18, 1988.

Montgomery, L. M. *Emily Climbs*, pp. 3–4. New York: HarperCollins, 1925/1953.

Murphy, Elizabeth. *The Developing Child*. Palo Alto, CA: Consulting Psychologists Press, 1992.

Myers, Isabel Briggs with Peter B. Myers. *Gifts Differing,* pp. 150–152. Palo Alto, CA: Consulting Psychologists Press, 1993.

Myers, Isabel Briggs. *Introduction to Type* (5th ed.). Palo Alto,CA: Consulting Psychologists Press, 1993.

Myers, Isabel Briggs and Mary H. McCaulley. *Manual: A Guide to the Development and Use of the Myers-Briggs Type Indicator.* Palo Alto, CA: Consulting Psychologists Press, 1985.

Neider, Charles, ed. *The Autobiography of Mark Twain,* pp. 288–289. New York: HarperCollins, 1959.

Oates, Stephen B. *Let the Trumpet Sound: The Life of Martin Luther King, Jr.,* p. 56. New York: HarperCollins, 1982.

Oates, Stephen B. *With Malice Toward None: The Life of Abraham Lincoln,* p. 264. New York: HarperCollins, 1977.

Parini, Jay. "In Restaurants, a Writer Finds, the Muse Is Never Far Away," *The Chronicle of Higher Education,* November 7, 1990, p. B1.

Partington, Angela, ed. *The Oxford Dictionary of Quotations* (4th ed.). New York: Oxford University Press, 1992.

Peck, M. Scott. *The Road Less Traveled,* pp. 258–259. New York: Simon & Schuster, 1978.

Quenk, Naomi. *Beside Ourselves: Our Hidden Personality in Everyday Life.* Palo Alto, CA: Consulting Psychologists Press, 1993.

Rohman, Gordon. "Prewriting: The Stage of Discovery in the Writing Process," *College Composition and Communication,* 16 (1965): pp. 106–112.

Rose, Mike. "Rigid Rules, Inflexible Plans, and the Stifling of Language: A Cognitivist Analysis of Writer's Block." *College Composition and Communication,* 31 (1980): pp. 389–401.

Salinger, J. D. *Catcher in the Rye,* p. 184. New York: Bantam Books, 1951.

Saunders, Frances W. *Katherine and Isabel: Mother's Light, Daughter's Journey,* pp. 82–83. Palo Alto, CA: Consulting Psychologists Press, 1991.

Scanlon, Susan. "Writing Your Natural Way," *The Type Reporter,* 1990, Vol. 4, Nos. 8–12 and Vol. 5, No. 1.

Selzer, Richard. "The Pen and the Scalpel," *New York Times Magazine,* August 21, 1988, pp. 30, 31.

Simons, Marlise. "Love and Age: A Conversation With Garcia Marquez," *New York Times Book Review,* April 7, 1985, p. 18.

Smith, Frank. *Writing and the Writer,* p. 5. New York: Holt, Rinehart and Winston, 1982.

Steinbeck, John. *Travels with Charlie in Search of America,* p. 11. New York: Bantam Books, 1962.

Sweetman, David. *Mary Renault: A Biography.* New York: Harcourt Brace Jovanovich, 1993.

Tuchman, Barbara. *Practicing History,* p. 37. New York: Knopf, 1981.

Tyler, Anne. *The Accidental Tourist,* p. 11. New York: Knopf, 1985.

Tyler, Anne. "Writers in Place and Writers in Motion." Review of Claudia Tate's *Black Women Writers at Work, New York Times Book Review,* May 29, 1983, p. 15.

"Updike on Updike." *Page One.* Interview, December 3, 1987. Public Relations, Saint Louis University, p. 1.

Walters, Marianne, Betty Carter, Peggy Papp, and Olga Silverstein. *The Invisible Web: Gender Patterns in Family Relations,* p. 10. New York: Guilford, 1988.

Weber, Bruce. "The Myth Maker: The Creative Mind of Novelist E. L. Doctorow," *New York Times Magazine,* October 20, 1985, p. 42.

Winokur, Jon. *Writers on Writing* (2d ed.). Philadelphia: Running Press, 1987.

Credits

Page x From *Writing and the Writer* by Frank Smith, pp. 5, 70. New York: Holt, Rinehart and Winston, 1982. Copyright 1982 by Frank Smith. Reprinted by permission. **12** From "The Open Classroom" by Herbert R. Kohl, *The New York Review of Books,* 1969. Copyright © 1969 by Nyrev, Inc. Reprinted with permission from *The New York Review of Books.* **28** From "In Restaurants, A Writer Finds, the Muse is Never Far Away" by Jay Parini, *The Chronicle of Higher Education,* November 7, 1990, B1. Copyright 1990 by Jay Parini. Reprinted by permission. **30** From *The Writing Life* by Annie Dillard, pp. 26, 31, 79. New York: Harper Perennial, 1989. Copyright 1989 by HarperCollins. Reprinted by permission. **32** From *Winston Churchill: The Last Lion (Alone 1932–40)* Vol. 2 by William Manchester, pp. 11, 33. Boston: Little, Brown, 1988. Copyright © 1988 by William Manchester. By permission of Little, Brown and Company. **33** From "Braver Than We Thought" by E. L. Doctorow. Review of Ernest Hemingway's *The Garden of Eden, New York Times Book Review,* May 18, 1986, pp. 1, 44. Copyright 1986 by *New York Times.* Reprinted by permission. **33** From "Revision and Life: Take It From the Top—Again" by Nora Ephron, *New York Times Book Review,* November 9, 1986, p. 7. Copyright 1986 by *New York Times.* Reprinted by permission. **34** From "The Need to Say It" by Patricia Hampl. In *The Writer on Her Work.* Vol. 2, *New Essays in New Territory,* edited by Janet Sternberg, pp. 21–22. New York: Norton, 1991. Copyright 1991 by Norton. **34** From "Updike on Updike," an interview in *Page One* on December 3, 1987, p. 1, by the Public Relations Department of Saint Louis University. Copyright 1987 by Saint Louis University. Reprinted by permission. **39** From review of James A. Michener's *The Novel* by Susan Isaacs, *New York Times Book Review,* March 31, 1991, p.12. Copyright 1991 by *New York Times.* Reprinted by permission. **41** From "The Myth Maker: The Creative Mind of Novelist E. L. Doctorow" by Bruce Weber, *New York Times Magazine,* October 20, 1985, p. 42. Copyright 1985 by *New York Times Magazine.* Reprinted by permission. **49** From "Styron's Choices" by Philip Caputo, *Esquire,* December, 1986, p. 152. Reprinted by permission. **51, 62** From "The Pen and the Scalpel" by Richard Selzer, *New York Times Magazine,* August 21, 1988, pp. 30, 31. Copyright 1988 by *New York Times Magazine.* Reprinted by permission. **52** From *Emily Climbs* by L. M. Montgomery, pp.3–4. New York: HarperCollins, 1925/1953. Copyright 1925 by Harper Collins. Reprinted by permission. **53, 59** From *Let the Trumpet Sound: The Life of Martin Luther King, Jr.* by Stephen B. Oates, p. 56. New York:

Index